CENTURION
P R I N C I P L E

....
THE PROTOCOL OF AUTHORITY
....

★ NEIL KENNEDY ★

The Centurion Principle
Copyright © 2008 by Neil Kennedy

EDITOR: Linda A. Schantz

Neil Kennedy Ministries Group
82 Plantation Pointe
Fairhope, AL 36532

3rd EDITION
First Printed in November 2008

www.fivestarman.com
www.neilkennedyministries.com

Dedication

This book is dedicated to my family, who has entrusted me with their lives, honored me with their commitment, and made me proud of their dedication.

It is also dedicated to those whom I have served and to those who have served me within the protocol of authority. Wisdom is gained through mentorship or through pain.

Thank you to those who have invested in me.

Table of Contents

.

Introduction

Let's be honest. Most of us deal with authority issues.

To prove my point, let's take a pop-quiz.

You're driving on the road and look ahead to see blue lights flashing. A police officer is behind a car that he has pulled over. If you immediately have sympathetic thoughts for the person who was pulled over, you have authority issues.

Don't worry. You're not alone.

The *principle of authority* is a New Testament concept. The Old Testament has only two references regarding the word *authority* itself. The first reference is in the Book of Esther, when Mordecai instituted the Jewish festival of Purim because he had *overpowered* his adversary (*Esther 9:29*). The word *authority* literally means *overpowered* in this reference.

The second reference to the word *authority* in the Old Testament is found in the Book of Proverbs.

> *When the righteous are in authority, the people rejoice: but when the wicked beareth rule, the people mourn.*
>
> *Proverbs 29:2*

In this verse the word translated as *authority* means *to be or to become great; to be or to become many;* or simply *numerous.* It is the authority of the masses. When the righteous have become numerous there is much to celebrate.

The New Testament is predominantly where you'll find the teaching of *authority*. In fact, the most remarkable notation people made concerning Jesus' teaching is that "He taught as one having authority" *(Matthew 7:29)*. This clearly distinguished Him as being different from the other teachers of His time. The teaching and miracle ministry of Jesus exercised by authority is one of His most defining attributes. After healing the paralytic in Matthew 9 by announcing the forgiveness of sins, the teachers of the Law accused Jesus of blasphemy. They had authority issues.

Jesus answered their evil and slanderous accusations saying, "So you may know that the Son of Man has authority on earth to forgive sins…," and then He promptly turned to the paralytic and said, "Get up, take your mat and go home." The man was instantly healed, and the crowd rejoiced and praised God who had given such authority to men.

Notice, the crowd recognized that the authority Jesus exercised was not limited to Him alone, but that it was also given to *men*—meaning *mankind*. Mankind was given authority at Creation *(see Genesis 1:26)*; however, man forfeited the position of authority due to disobedience. The Gospel of Christ reestablished the proper protocol of man's authority.

The word *authority* causes many people to cringe with haunting memories of the past or the anticipation of abuse. In our day, much authority has been misused for personal gain. Power is often manipulated for self-promotion and exercised for control and dictatorial oppression.

I have spoken to hundreds of people who are gripped with agonizing mental pain due to abused authority. Many parents, teachers, attorneys, coaches, clergy, and politicians have misused the hand of authority to hurt rather than heal, to abuse rather than comfort, to molest rather than motivate.

Obviously, this is not the New Testament idea of authority that Jesus practiced or promoted. Jesus taught the very opposite use of authority. In Matthew 20:25, Jesus said, "You know that the rulers of the Gentiles lord it over them, and their high officials exercise authority over them. Not so with you." The principle of authority that Jesus taught is the use of Servant Leadership. Servant Leadership is when a leader properly understands that his position *under* authority gives him responsibility for the things he is placed *over*.

True authority is having the legitimate right to use power.

Most people confuse *power* with *authority*. A person who has a firearm can have the *power* to shoot it, but he doesn't necessarily have the *authority* to do so. True authority is having the legitimate right to use power. Moses was described in the Bible as "the meekest man on the earth," yet his leadership provides us with a clear example of more authority than any other man in the Old Testament. True meekness is not weakness; it is actually *strength submitted to authority*.

We need authority. We need the protection authority provides. We need to have established authorities in our lives so that we may prosper and experience godly promotion. Without authority we have anarchy, turmoil, and disorder. The godly use of authority is the need of the hour. It is imperative that we regain an understanding of this principle.

A servant leader understands that his position under authority makes him responsible for the things he is placed over.

We're living in treacherous times. Hidden and unpredictable dangers are everywhere around us. In the world today, we face the constant threat of terrorism, which is the use of violence and intimidation against established authorities. We attempt to appease tyrants in hostile nations who are bartering with our enemies for nuclear weapons. Politicians are misusing their entrusted powers to further their own personal ambitions. Even ecclesiastical figures see themselves more as attorneys prosecuting God's justice, rather than serving as agents of His divine grace.

We are surrounded by anarchists and schemers, polluting their own bodies with perversions, slandering celestial powers, and behaving with total contempt of what is right. They are "shepherds who feed only themselves" *(Jude 12)*.

Although the abuses are global, what hits more at home for most of us individually is the misunderstood and misused purpose of authority in the lives of husbands and fathers.

Absentee fatherhood is a cultural epidemic which has repercussions that cannot be measured merely by statistics. Its impact is seen in the lives of young men turning to uncontrolled violence and in young women by the molestation of their dignity. Countless fatherless boys, lacking a model of manhood, never grow into masculinity, but denying their natural state, they choose to become effeminate. *(See Romans 1:27.)* Many fatherless girls, missing a true gentleman's affirmation, misuse their physical beauty to attract male attention, no matter how abusive and improper it may be. Wives, longing for the security and comfort of a strong man in the household, become repulsed by their weak, emotive, whining, "Momma's-boy" husbands. Some are figuratively "wearing the pants" of a man, fearful of exposing themselves to this world without some line of defense.

There is a combative enmity between the woman and Satan, the enemy of our souls. *(See Genesis 3:15.)* Without the model of authority of a godly man—whether it be a father or a husband— young women are exposed to harassment and helplessness.

I know this isn't politically correct in our time of feministic idealism, but I believe that men must become real men and step into their proper roles to fulfill God's plan for the family—not to return to the old ideas of male chauvinism, or to adopt the Latin ideas of machismo, but to become servant leaders to our wives, to our children, to the church, and to the community at large.

Feminism is much like communism. It is an extreme reaction to the abuse of an authoritative system run amok.

It is imperative that men step up to their God-assigned positions of authority—not to oppress, manipulate, control, or subvert—but to serve. It is time for men to redefine the perception of masculinity.

This will not be an easy task in our day of beer-gutted buffoons who function as the leading examples of men on television, humoring the always-more-intelligent women of the household. It will be a challenge to overcome the popularly idealized male role model as a metro-sexual, pretty-boy with effeminate traits. As society emasculates men, we must gird up our loins to defend our created purpose.

I am not espousing the idea of a male dictator whose idea of strength is to beat a woman or oppress his subservients. I'm talking about a man who leads by the strength of his character and protects by the courage of his convictions.

In the next few chapters, I will address the Protocol of Authority; how authority flows through leadership, not around it. I will discuss the proper attitude of approaching authority, how to become a person of authority, and the privileges afforded to those who lead others with authority.

As an example, we will use a man who literally astonished Jesus. This man is distinguished among all of Israel because of his personal understanding of authority. The Centurion, trained in the military sciences, leading others with great humility, used his position not for personal gain, but for the honor of those he served above him and the benefit of those who served beneath him.

It is my deepest desire that this book will equip you with the understanding that authority exists in your life to empower, protect, promote, and prosper those who are a part of your world. Godly authority gives you the ability to manage your responsibilities and to walk with the dignity of manhood, the intellect of wisdom, and the controlled meekness of a true leader.

SECTION 1
Serving Under Authority

Chapter 1
The Centurion Principle

When Jesus had entered Capernaum, a centurion came to him, asking for help. "Lord," he said, "my servant lies at home paralyzed and in terrible suffering."

Jesus said to him, "I will go and heal him."

The centurion replied, "Lord, I do not deserve to have you come under my roof. But just say the word, and my servant will be healed. For I myself am a man under authority, with soldiers under me. I tell this one, 'Go,' and he goes; and that one, 'Come,' and he comes. I say to my servant, 'Do this,' and he does it."

When Jesus heard this, he was astonished and said to those following him, "I tell you the truth, I have not found anyone in Israel with such great faith. I say to you that many will come from the East and the West, and will take their places at the feast with Abraham, Isaac, and Jacob in the kingdom of heaven. But the subjects of the kingdom will be thrown outside, into the darkness, where there will be weeping and gnashing of teeth."

Then Jesus said to the centurion, "Go! It will be done just as you believed it would." And his servant was healed at that very hour.

Matthew 8:5–13

A centurion of Jesus' day was a strong man—a "man's man," so to speak. He was physically conditioned and strong, able to carry 90 pounds of equipment up to 30 miles a day. His strength came from hardening his body. His very presence was impressive and imposing. He was the kind of man who overwhelmed the room. Others spoke softly around him. He was intimidating, yet reassuring, to the insecure and feeble. He was attractive, but not in the soft-skinned, boyish sense. This man's attractiveness was chiseled by seasons of facing challenges and overcoming obstacles.

He had intellectual training. As a student and teacher, he was able to read, write, and clearly articulate his thoughts. He was not given to exaggeration or the embellishment of his accomplishments. The medals on his chest were awarded for his discipline, not bought to fulfill his egocentric fantasies.

Schooled in the military sciences, the centurion was also trained in leadership skills, being able to manage 80–100 men. The best of the best were promoted to lead cohorts of 400–800 legionnaires, including other centurions.

A centurion was a professional officer in the Roman army, a seasoned man of at least 30 years of age. To become a centurion required the recommendation of, and several letters from, important people, including senators and dignitaries. Therefore, a centurion was well influenced, had strong relationships, and possessed a hierarchal blood line.

Dressed in silver armor accented by the bright colors of Italian fashion, the centurion distinguished himself. He walked with dignity, knowing that he represented the greatest army in the history of the world. Even in our day, all the United States military branches find their roots in the military sciences of ancient Rome because of its efficient mastery of the art of combat.

Centurions conditioned themselves for crisis. They hardened themselves—not for the sake of bitterness, but for the sake of strength. They knew that the display of strength actually helped them to *avoid* conflict. They demonstrated their strength in their demeanor, not with arrogance but with dignity. Centurions were strong men with well-trained minds and armored emotions.

The centurion exhibited a very different standard than today's display of emotive, wimpy, fools on parade. We have become weakened by the cowardice of idiots who are willing to strap on a bomb to blow themselves up to kill women and children. Some late-night television personalities would rather give up our liberties than courageously face the reality of evil. They argue for "peace" at all costs, rather than echo the shouts of our forefathers, "freedom at any cost!" This great country was built on the same moral values as those of the centurion, willing to fight—willing to die for our freedoms.

> *We need men to rise up—to be proud of their positions of leadership—and to be determined to protect, promote, and prosper those under their authority.*

The centurion was a man who stood tall with the honor of his convictions. He was not bent over or weakened by crisis. We need men to stand up tall and become men who are willing to courageously face the challenges of our time.

This is the kind of man who approached Jesus.

For the centurion to approach Jesus on behalf of his servant also required a sense of humility. The centurion in Matthew 8 was a Gentile, yet he was willing to approach a Jewish man, a man who was under the occupied control of the Roman Empire. In all reality, the centurion was of much greater social hierarchy than Jesus was, yet he showed meekness in addressing the Lord.

As strong, conditioned, and influential as the centurion was, he faced a challenge for which he needed help. It is apparent in scripture that his young servant had been injured, paralyzed in some way. Luke, the physician states that he was very sick and on the verge of death. *(See Luke 7:3.)* Obviously, it was a crisis moment—one that required immediate and unusual action. This was the reason that the centurion called upon Jesus. He valued his young servant highly. He cared for his well-being.

The heart of a leader is to care about those beneath him. Because of this, the centurion, with respect for the practice of protocol, used his influence to seek out the One who could help him.

(Influence is a currency—a medium of exchange. For a detailed teaching on this topic, please see my book entitled, God's Currency.)

The Protocol of Authority

The centurion understood proper protocol. He approached Jesus for help, while respecting the position of Jesus' authority. The centurion showed his understanding of protocol by addressing Jesus with the title conveying his utmost respect, "Lord."

This is very different from others who approached Jesus. The Pharisees and Sadducees addressed Jesus with a lower title and a tone of disrespect, calling Him, "Teacher." Normally, this title would be considered adequate if one was addressing an itinerant rabbi, but the religious leaders of Jesus' day used it to scorn Jesus, rather than to honor Him. It's much like when a person addresses a minister, calling him, "Preacher" today.

The centurion's address signifies that he submitted to the *supremacy* of Jesus. He recognized that Jesus was the "possessor and disposer" of the power that he needed.

Many people make this mistake when they approach God the Father in prayer. They do not practice proper protocol. Jesus taught the principle of approaching God with propriety when He showed us how to pray.

> *This, then, is how you should pray: "Our Father in heaven, hallowed be your name, your kingdom come, your will be done on earth as it is in heaven. Give us today our daily bread. Forgive us our debts, as we also have forgiven our debtors. And lead us not into temptation, but deliver us from the evil one."*
>
> *Matthew 6:9–13*

When Jesus said, "Hallowed be your name," He used this form of address to acknowledge that His Father had the highest status in the position of protocol. He approached the Father in Heaven, under the position of His own name. The name of Jesus has been set apart as having authority above all things, yet Jesus approached the Heavenly Father supremely honoring the name of the Father even above His own name.

Jesus said, "My Father will give you whatever you ask in my *name*. Until now you have not asked for anything in my *name*" *(John 16:23, emphasis added)*.

The name of Jesus is the only name for the salvation of man. "Salvation is found in no one else, for there is *no other name* under heaven given to men by which we must be saved" *(Acts 4:12, emphasis added)*.

The world has shown disdain toward the name of Jesus, yet it is the name by which man must be saved. Comedians use the name of Jesus to shock their audiences, thinking that their vile rants somehow position them as intellectual, yet proving their ignorance. No other name can separate the culture like the name of Jesus.

Capitalizing the *U* in *universe*, the *B* in *being*, the *S* in *supreme*, or the *D* in *deity* will not usher you into the presence of the Father. We have one, and *only* one way to the Father, and that is through the gate of Jesus. Jesus said, "I am the gate; whoever enters through me will be saved" *(John 10:9)*.

The reverse is also true. Just as Jesus is the gate to the Father, Jesus is also the Father's gate to us. This is an important truth that we will explore later. For now, notice that the centurion practiced protocol when approaching Jesus.

Chapter 2

Servant Leadership

When Jesus had entered Capernaum, a centurion came to him, asking for help. "Lord," he said, "my servant lies at home paralyzed and in terrible suffering."

Jesus said to him, "I will go and heal him."

Matthew 8:5–7

The centurion made his request on behalf of his servant. This is servant leadership.

In our day, few leaders understand the value of those who diligently serve them. Many leaders see their employees merely as disposable property, useful only for their own selfish ambitions. "Easy come, easy go," seems to be the mentality. Some are flippant when it comes to the value of "lower-level" people, while they esteem themselves as indispensable.

We've all heard the disparaging remarks of the arrogant elite. We've all seen imperious leaders look with disdain toward their "hired help" in a disgusting performance of pride and self-grandeur.

The political arena is overwhelmed with men veneered with righteousness who are only masking their self-serving vanity. Business leaders are ruthless in their aspirations to climb the corporate ladder, justifying any unethical conduct as long as it causes their personal advancement. The means always justifies the end for these leaders.

Unfortunately, the Church is not immune to this egocentric attitude, for it has made its way into the conduct of some Christian leaders. In our world, it seems that many preachers are more motivated to surround themselves with an entourage rather than disciples.

This depravity is better left to the seedy underbelly of society like the Mafia, not in the halls of government, the board rooms of corporations, or the sanctuaries of our churches. We should not be forced to watch the "Godfather" series in order to conduct business meetings. This kind of attitude is more akin to Civil War Era plantation owners who ruled by intimidation and torture, motivating workers with the whip of terror.

This calloused and embittered reaction toward people is obviously not the attitude that God takes concerning us.

The centurion demonstrated such dignity in his leadership skills. It is honorable how he cared for the young servant under his authority.

The Benefits of Servant Leadership

"Praise the Lord, O my soul, and forget not all his benefits."
Psalm 103:2

When submitting to authority, a person should know the benefits of doing so. Few people realize the benefits of authority. So many have been abused by so-called authorities in their lives that they have a negative reflex to anyone who tries to exercise authority over them.

I'm not advocating submission to wicked authoritarians who endeavor to oppress their subservients; however, **submission to God-ordained authority provides blessings which bring promotion to those who comply.**

I do believe we should observe established authorities to determine if they are legitimately using their leadership. We can recognize authentic authority by:

1. The Benefit of Power—One Greek synonym for authority is *energeia,* which means *superhuman power.* Authority above you should give you power that you do not possess on your own. Jesus received all authority. Then He transferred that authority to his followers *(Matthew 28:17–19).*

2. The Benefit of Protection—Another synonym for authority is *exousia,* which means *to rule and cover with protection.* Legitimate authority shelters and protects those who serve under it *(Psalm 91:1).* Jesus referred to the people of Israel as sheep without a shepherd, indicating that although they had established leadership, their leadership did not have authority. Matthew 7:29 says, "The crowds were amazed at [Jesus'] teaching, because He taught as one who had authority, and not as their teachers."

3. The Benefit of Provision—The synonym for authority, *dunamis,* means *power and influence which belong to riches and wealth.* 1 Corinthians 9:7 asks, "Who serves as a soldier at his own expense?" When you are placed securely under authority you should draw provision.

4. The Benefit of Promotion—*Ishus* is a synonym which denotes *ability* or *force.* The natural process of following great leaders should result in becoming better by default. Proverbs says, "He who walks with the wise grows wise." Jesus said, "Come, follow me and I will make you…" *(Matthew 4:19).*

Authority in your life should not use manipulation or control to lead you. You should have no sense of intimidation or insecurity while serving a leader. In fact, you should have a sense of confidence, respect, and motivation if you are submitted to legitimate authority. These are the qualities that the centurion in Matthew 8 demonstrated as he approached Jesus.

The Imposition of the Request

Upon hearing the condition of the centurion's servant, Jesus offered to help, saying, "I will go and heal him."

The centurion continued to show incredible insight concerning protocol. He looked at the imposition that Jesus would have suffered by going to his home. The Jews had a tradition that Jesus would have to break to enter the house of the centurion and restore his servant to health. A Gentile's home was considered unclean by the Orthodox standard. Jesus said that the Pharisees, "nullify the Word of God for the sake of tradition" *(Matthew 15:6)*.

Jesus was willing to break the traditions of men to keep the commands of God. He certainly did so by healing on the Sabbath and by eating grain while walking through the fields on the Sabbath. Jesus taught that man is the "Lord" of the Sabbath, not under its supremacy.

In any case, the centurion carefully considered the imposition of his request.

When you serve a person of authority, you should respect their position. You should honor it.

In 1999, while serving another man, I received an invitation to a meeting in Dallas, Texas. Those invited to the meeting were the most influential Christian leaders of the day. Although I was not one of the influential leaders, I served a man who was in those ranks. My invitation came because of him.

The letter gave me the rules of conduct that I needed to know—what time I should arrive, the attire, the length of the meeting, and the confidentiality of the event.

The day came, and we arrived in Dallas for the meeting. In the room, men began to position themselves for the meeting. The Secret Service began to scan the room as, then Governor, George W. Bush walked into the room. He was making his bid for the White House, and we were there to ask him questions that pertained to our interests.

As he entered the room, he shook a few hands and then made a beeline straight to me. I was standing in the back of the room away from the line. I was simply observing the activities, when he passed everyone, approached me, made eye-contact, and stuck out his hand to greet me. "Hi, I'm, George W."

For the next few seconds, I looked directly at him. Watching his lips moving, I couldn't hear anything that he was saying. As I stood there, my spirit spoke very loudly to me, *"Neil, practice protocol."*

Standing near me was the man whom I served.

I knew immediately what I should do. It was not right for me to grip and seize the moment. It was inappropriate for me to hoard it. My position—my responsibility—was to take a step back, and introduce Governor Bush to my leader.

When his lips stopped moving, I politely turned and practiced protocol. When I did, I stepped out of the way so that the two of them could have a conversation.

It was the only meeting I ever had with President Bush. It was probably a once-in-a-lifetime experience. Yet, it was also my responsibility to show respect in my position.

When you are under leadership, you should consider the imposition of your demands upon it. You should esteem your leaders highly. You should show preference for your superiors.

This is the example that Jesus modeled during His agonizing surrender in the Garden of Gethsemane. He prayed, "My Father, if it is possible, may this cup be taken from me. Yet not as I will, but as you will" *(Matthew 26:39)*.

Jesus' request displayed His respect toward the imposition upon the leadership of the Father. He preferred His Father's will above His own.

> *Your attitude should be the same as that of Christ Jesus: Who, being in very nature God, did not consider equality with God something to be grasped, but made himself nothing...*
>
> Philippians 2:5–7

Jesus did not grasp for His rights. He did not seize hold of position. Everything within the flesh of Jesus cried out against the looming pain that was approaching Him, yet He willingly submitted to the leadership of the Father's will.

Chapter 3

Serving at the Highest Level

Wives submit to your husbands as unto the Lord.

Ephesians 5:22

Submission is required when your personal desires and interests disagree with your willingness to follow leadership. Accepting and yielding to the protocol of authority is the act of submission.

Few people like the sound of the word *submission*. Our flesh resists the very thought of losing control or relinquishing our rights. It requires a tremendous amount of trust and confidence in the character of leadership above us to submit.

Most people rebel when they face the embarrassment of submission. Their pride causes them to abstain from humbling themselves and relinquishing their rights to accept the will of the authority above them.

Ephesians 5:22–23 uses the word *submit* to give us an example of serving at the highest level: *"Wives, submit to your husbands as unto the Lord. For the husband is the head of the wife…"*

The word *submit* in this verse is *hypotasso,* a Greek military term meaning, *to align in proper order in a military fashion under the command of a leader.* It means that the wife is under the servant leadership of her husband and that she is positioned for authority to work correctly in her life.

Submission is required when your personal desires and interests disagree with your willingness to follow leadership.

Notice that the wife is to *"submit to her husband as unto the Lord."* Doing so aligns her underneath the authoritative lineage of the Lord Jesus. She is submitted to the highest level through her husband, which brings her the greatest reward. As she submits to her husband, she is also submitted to the Lord Himself. Her submission also properly aligns her to manage what she is over.

Do not jump to conclusions. I am not suggesting that a wife is to submit to ungodly behavior from her husband. If he has the character of a centurion, he will serve his wife in his leadership. Colossians 3:19 admonishes, "Husbands, love your wives and do not be harsh with them." Husbands should not embitter their wives, nor should they prick them with derogatory words.

A wife should be able to trust the character of her husband. She should be completely confident that her husband is not only willing to serve her in his leadership, but that he is also willing to die for her protection. This will allow her to experience the total security that comes with servant leadership.

I see men who are constantly irritating their wives. It is as if they feel empowered if they can exasperate the weaker vessel. To *exasperate* means *to arise anger in someone as a form of punishment.* Some men seem to find pleasure in causing their wives mental anguish through the instability of their relationships. They say, "I want to keep her guessing." That kind of relationship is akin to a juvenile crush in a schoolyard.

A husband should treat his wife with the utmost dignity and love toward her. Why would you treat a woman any other way?

Serving as Unto the Lord

Serving at the highest level is the proper protocol of submission. When a wife is serving her husband as unto the Lord, it means that her behavior is admirable when her husband is with her or when he is absent. His eyes do not have to be upon her constantly to keep her "in check."

Likewise, when an employee serves at the highest level, he is consistent in his performance whether he is monitored by his superiors or not. *The Message* Bible expresses this very well:

> *Servants, respectfully obey your earthly masters but always with an eye to obeying the real master, Christ. Don't just do what you have to do to get by, but work heartily, as Christ's servants doing what God wants you to do. And work with a smile on your face, always keeping in mind that no matter who happens to be giving the orders, you're really serving God. Good work will get you good pay from the Master, regardless of whether you are slave or free.*
>
> *Ephesians 6:5–8 MSG*

The employee who fulfills this passage is the kind of person that you can't keep down. He can't be hidden. His gifts are too evident to be relegated to the back room in obscurity.

> *Do you see a man skilled in his work? He will serve before kings; he will not serve before obscure men.*
>
> *Proverbs 22:29*

You cannot hide a skilled person. The gift within him promotes him. His gift makes a way for him. It opens doors. It is like a magnet. Skilled people can't be held down.

I recently met a man named Bruce who retired in the small bayside community where I live. I'd seen him several times in the local UPS store where I ship out the products and books that my companies produce. Bruce is the father-in-law of the owner of the store. Bruce's story demonstrates how skill will elevate a man out of obscurity. As a young man, he got a temporary job at UPS loading trucks. His diligence and skill lifted him through the company ranks to serve as regional manager.

Bruce obviously was an intelligent man but he also proved faithful to serve at every level of the organization. I ran into Bruce and his wife in the Atlanta airport a few weeks ago, they were returning from Greece. They are enjoying five or six trips a year. They live in a beautiful home on the Bay of Mobile, where the sunsets are spectacular. Life is good for them now because Bruce learned the principle that skill elevates you out of obscurity.

When you serve the highest level, you position yourself for promotion. When change comes to the leadership above you, you are protected by your proper alignment. If your immediate supervisor is drafted up, he will take you with him because of your work ethic and loyalty to him. If your immediate superior is removed, you will be drafted into his place because you were not just serving his leadership, you were serving the top of the organization through his leadership and even beyond it.

Serving at the highest level gives you security beyond the company that you presently serve. It is as if you are literally employed by God and not merely by man. Promotion doesn't come from man. It comes from the Lord (Psalm 75:6–7).

This is a vital principle to incorporate into your life. It will guarantee that you are always secure in your employment, no matter what the turbulence is around you.

> *He will have no fear of bad news; his heart is steadfast, trusting in*
> *the Lord.*
>
> Psalm 112:7

You will also be protected if you witness activity that is unethical, or even criminal. Having the security that you not only serve with honor toward your immediate supervisor but serving unto the Lord will give you the confidence that you need to keep from compromising.

In 2001, a senior employee approached her superior with the revelation that accounting irregularities would cause their company to crumble into ruin. When Sherron Watkins confronted CEO Kenneth Lay, she did so with confidence that she was honoring a superior position of authority—the authority of integrity. She knew that she must serve the principles of integrity above any man. Although others compromised their integrity, she knew that her confrontation would put a chain reaction in motion that revealed Enron's façade. She did not cause the downward spiral of unethical behavior, she simply revealed the unethical decisions that would do so.

A great example in the Bible of serving at the highest level is how David protected his father's sheep as a shepherd boy. That is what eventually promoted him to serve under the king.

> *David said to Saul, "Your servant has been keeping his father's sheep.*
> *When a lion or a bear came and carried off a sheep from the flock, I went*
> *after it, struck it and rescued the sheep from its mouth. When it turned on*
> *me, I seized it by its hair, struck it and killed it. Your servant has killed*
> *both the lion and the bear; this uncircumcised Philistine will be like one*

*of them, because he has defied the armies of the living God. The Lord who
delivered me from the paw of the lion and the paw of the bear will deliver
me from the hand of this Philistine." Saul said to David, "Go, and the
Lord be with you."*

I Samuel 17:34–37

The Israeli Army was on the battle lines to face the dreaded Philistines. The warrior of the Philistines, Goliath, was a champion in battle. He was massive physically and highly skilled in warfare. Not only was he skilled in the use of spears, swords, and shields, but he was also skilled in psychological warfare. He used intimidation techniques and caused many mighty warriors to cower.

David arrived on the scene merely to deliver his brothers' lunch, when he overheard Goliath's arrogant blasphemies. The vileness of the giant's pride was repulsive to David. Looking around, David saw the army of God quivering with cowardice.

David was full of faith. "I can do this," he said. His confidence didn't come from presumption. David's confidence was a God confidence. Knowing that he served the Living God and was underneath His authority gave David the faith that he would be able to win the battle.

Most people presume that they have faith. They live their lives, handling their own affairs, relying solely upon themselves. When a challenge comes that overwhelms them, they try to believe God. They call for His authority to work in their lives. Not only is this presumptuous, but it also usually proves to be disastrous.

Having faith in God is simply believing that He is faithful to His Word. To have complete confidence in His Word, we must learn to prove Him in the small challenges. Then when a crisis arises we will be prepared to handle it. If we can't rely upon God's Word and prove Him for a headache, we will not have the faith we need if we must battle a life-threatening disease. If you don't trust His voice to give you direction in daily traffic, how will you receive His leading when He speaks to you about your destiny?

David had proven his reliance on God's authority in his life when he fought the lion and wrestled the bear. He knew that the giant would be no different from them. His confidence was upon the supernatural power of God and the simple techniques that he had mastered in battle.

Never attempt to face a challenge without proven skills.

King Saul was a head taller than any of the other Israelites. He was the man closest to the giant's size in Israel. Saul should have been the one to step out and face the giant. As the nation's leader, it was his responsibility. Rather than standing firm in his authority, Saul offered David, the small, ruddy young man, his oversized armor. David tried it on for size.

> *"I cannot go in these," he said to Saul, "because I am not used to them."*
>
> *I Samuel 17:39*

Never attempt to face a challenge without proven skills. You already have the ability to overcome the challenges that you face. We have this assurance.

> *"God is faithful; he will not let you be tempted beyond what you can bear. But when you are tempted, he will also provide a way out so that you can stand up under it."*
>
> *I Corinthians 10:13*

The giant was obstinate. He was appalled that the challenger was such a poor match. The giant grunted out curses and insults.

> *"God chose the foolish things of the world to shame the wise; God chose the weak things of the world to shame the strong."*
>
> *I Corinthians 1:27*

David's confession of faith teaches a great lesson about serving at the highest level. David declared that he would decapitate the giant. He only walked out to meet the warrior with a sling and five stones, yet he prophesied that he would soon be shearing his head off!

> *This day the Lord will hand you over to me, and I'll strike you down and cut off your head. Today I will give the carcasses of the Philistine army to the birds of the air and the beasts of the earth, and the whole world will know that there is a God in Israel.*
>
> *I Samuel 17:46*

David's faith extended beyond facing the single great warrior to challenging the entire Philistine army.

When you face a crisis, you might as well claim total victory while you're at it. Don't stop short. Push through the challenge for a complete resolution. David's confidence was in the Lord as he declared, "The battle is the Lord's."

This is how you serve at the highest level. You can approach the crisis or the challenge as something that is beneath your authority *because of what is above you.*

Even though the giant towered over him, David knew that in the spirit realm, the giant was "subject" to him.

Serving at the highest level gives you mastery over what is beneath you.

Chapter 4
Serving a Hostile Leader

While we're looking into David's life, let's examine how to serve a hostile leader. David certainly knew a few things about that.

Some people today might argue, saying, "I don't mind serving under leadership, but the person I am serving is unethical—or mean,—or ruthless,—or simply incompetent."

What do you do when you are placed underneath a ruthless leader's authority?

You serve that person with loyalty.

I know what you're thinking—but there is a tremendous principle behind this mindset.

> *If you have not been trustworthy with someone else's property, who will give you property of your own?*
>
> Luke 16:12

Unless you are faithful with what is another man's, you do not qualify for your own.

After David's overwhelming defeat of Goliath, the Philistine army was routed by the Israelites. David, still holding the head of Goliath, was drafted by King Saul to stay with him. Jonathan, King Saul's son, was a noble man and a true prince. When Jonathan saw David he made a covenant with him. Jonathan gave his robe, tunic, belt, bow, and even his sword to David. Whether he knew it or not, Jonathan was prophesying that David would become the prince—the heir of the throne of Saul.

Unless you are faithful with what is another man's, you do not qualify for your own.

David proved successful in everything that Saul sent him to do. He was so successful that songs were written minimizing Saul and glorifying David. Obviously, this caused a bitter root to spring up in Saul's heart.

We've all seen this kind of transition before. A man works tirelessly to build something and to establish a company. His efforts are celebrated, until a young, fresh upstart takes it away from him. All of a sudden, the founder, the stalwart, is forgotten. No one remembers the pains and the challenges that he overcame to get the company to where it is. The charismatic youth takes the place of honor.

> *Better a poor but wise youth than an old but foolish king who no longer knows how to take warning. The youth may have come from prison to the kingship, or he may have been born in poverty within his kingdom. I saw that all who lived and walked under the sun followed the youth, the king's successor. There was no end to all the people who were before them. But those who came later were not pleased with the successor. This too is meaningless, a chasing after the wind.*
>
> *Ecclesiastes 4:13–16*

The cycle seems to never end. People don't remember what you have done. They only remain loyal to you for what they think you *will* do. It's *not,* "What have you done for me lately?" In actuality, it's more like, *"What will you promise to do for me next?"*

The 2008 presidential campaigns were marked by two themes; one touted "experience" while the other promised "change." When it comes to the masses' choice, they will choose change every time. They are not happy with their own lives, so if you will give them the "audacity of hope," you won't have to give them specifics. As long as you are charismatic on the delivery, the world will crown you as their leader.

Saul began to resent the very notion that the people—his people—were writing and singing songs about the young upstart, David. Saul became so embittered and angry that a forceful evil spirit began to direct his decisions.

Saul's bipolar episodes controlled him. One minute Saul was trying to pin David to a wall with a spear, the next minute he was saying, "I have sinned. Come back, David, my son. I've acted like a fool and have made a big mistake" *(I Samuel 26:21).*

Have you ever served someone so evil? Someone bent on your destruction?

If so, follow the example of David. David's attitude was, "Do not touch my anointed ones; do my prophets no harm" *(I Chronicles 16:22, Psalm 105:15).*

A few years ago, the Lord called me to establish a church in a remarkable city. The city was promoted as "a model city for America." When I heard this, I said, *"If it is a model city for America, then it should have a relevant, Spirit-filled, influential church in it."* I accepted the challenge.

At that point in my life, this was the greatest challenge I had ever faced. I was up against enormous opposition. It would require incredible financial strength to do what God had asked of me. It would also require a team of committed individuals to start this church. I recruited a team of sharp young ministers to go with me, and I began to transfer all the resources from my personal travel ministry and even my personal finances to get the job done.

I never imagined that my integrity would be questioned. I assumed that it was obvious that my motives were pure. I had invested all that I had into the project.

I have never been one to "poor mouth." I think it is unbecoming to whine about finances. Either I have faith that God has called me and will supply the provision or I don't, but I am not going to use manipulative tactics to get people to give money.

The opposition to build the church did not come from outside forces. I would have expected it from city officials or the community at large, but my strongest opponents came from those with whom I served in fellowship. Although we had much success, establishing a viable witness to the community, reaching hundreds of people, I found myself in a political quagmire.

> *Ruthless witnesses come forward; they question me on things I know nothing about.*
>
> *Psalm 35:11*

I began to get resistance from a man in leadership in the ministerial affiliation to which I was submitted. In his deceived thinking, this man accepted a slanderous accusation against me. He began to question my motives, my integrity, my character, and my very existence.

I told him, "What are your questions? I'll be happy to answer them."

He would only respond, "There are just questions…"

No matter how much I attempted to answer the questions he had, nothing would suffice. I supported my answers with documentation and evidence of my integrity. He simply dismissed them as insufficient. My name was slandered, my ministerial reputation was hurt. Until that time, I had never experienced this kind of religious resistance. I was naive, inexperienced, and ill-prepared to know how to resist this type of attack. When I was young and naive, I trusted. When I matured and became wise, I tested.

When I was young and naive I trusted, when I matured and became wise, I tested.

What is truly amazing to me, is that I respected this man. I admired his work ethic and had celebrated his victories in ministry. When he battled an illness, I fasted and prayed for his healing.

> *When they were ill, I put on sackcloth and humbled myself with fasting.*
> *When my prayers returned to me unanswered, I went about mourning as*
> *though for my friend or brother. I bowed my head in grief as though*
> *weeping for my mother.*
>
> *Psalm 35:13–14*

I tried to reason with him. I attempted in every way to show myself a faithful servant, yet he would not bend. Face to face, he would capitulate, and seem to understand what I was saying, but the moment that I left the room, his heart would quickly turn against me. He would hate me all the more.

The only resolution that I could come to was to completely remove myself from under his leadership. That required that I transfer my pastoral leadership to an associate and move out of the arena of my nemesis.

My counselors advised me to fight, even litigate, my cause for justice. However, the Scripture advised a different approach.

> *If any of you has a dispute with another, dare he take it before the*
> *ungodly for judgment instead of before the saints?*
>
> *I Corinthians 6:1*

I believe it is repulsive that those in the church are taking their cases to secular courts for litigation. It is one thing to litigate an attack from the secular world, such as property rights, zoning laws, etc., but to ask courts to decide internal spiritual affairs is a violation of God's Word.

My only option was to accept his judgment against me and walk away in peace, rather than remain in strife. The decision was hard, but I knew that this was a moment of destiny for me and my family. If I chose to take up my own defense, the likely outcome was that my children could be ruined, embittered against the ministry. I'd seen that before. I witnessed the children of pastors lost because of the abuse that people wrought against their parents. I could not allow that to happen to my family.

> *Slaves, submit yourselves to your masters with all respect, not only to*
> *those who are good and considerate, but also to those who are harsh.*
>
> *I Peter 2:18*

Harsh leadership doesn't give you an excuse to use ungodly practices as a means of revenge. You must always walk in integrity, as unto the Lord.

We serve through leadership—
not around it.

The principle to remember is this: We serve through leadership—not around it. By serving faithfully under harsh treatment a reward is set in motion on your behalf.

> *For it is commendable if a man bears up under the pain of unjust suffering because he is conscious of God. But how is it to your credit if you receive a beating for doing wrong and endure it? But if you suffer for doing good and you endure it, this is commendable before God. To this you were called, because Christ suffered for you, leaving you an example, that you should follow in his steps.*
>
> *I Peter 2:19–21*

To be conscious of God means that you make a decision to follow a godly course of action, even though it would be more pleasurable to follow another way. Moses made this type of decision when "he chose to be mistreated along with the people of God rather than to enjoy the pleasures of sin for a short time" *(Hebrews 11:25)*.

It is the same decision that people of faith made when they "were tortured and refused to be released, so that they might gain a better resurrection. Some faced jeers and flogging, while still others were chained and put in prison. They were stoned; they were sawed in two; they were put to death by the sword. They went about in sheepskins and goatskins, destitute, persecuted, and mistreated—the world was not worthy of them" *(Hebrews 11:35–38)*.

Certainly, this is a higher level of living. A level of righteousness that few of us aspire to; yet we should. We should be willing to face harsh treatment for what is right.

John McCain lives the Centurion Principle. During the Vietnam war, he nearly lost his life in a fire on the U.S.S. Forrestal. In that same year, he was captured by the North Vietnamese. He spent more than five years as a P.O.W. in the famed Hanoi Hilton. With fractured legs and arms, his captors crushed his shoulder with a rifle butt, bayoneted him, and interrogated him without addressing his injuries. He spent two years in solitary confinement. When the ruthless men discovered that his father was a top admiral who had been named Commander of all U.S. Forces in the Vietnam theater, John McCain was offered a release.

Wanting to use him as a bargaining chip in their propaganda, the Vietnamese offered the young lieutenant freedom. McCain chose to remain under the harsh, inhuman treatment rather than accept a release offered to him in exchange for compromising his integrity.

The challenges that I have faced pale in comparison. I can't even be in the same room with the likes of John McCain when it comes to that kind of courage. But I do know that we all make the same choices to one degree or another. We must be strong in character and do what is right and what is noble, being ever conscious of our Lord.

When you face rejection, and even hostile opposition from those in authority over you, remain faithful and work diligently. God will not allow you to serve in obscurity. He will promote you.

Chapter 5

The Closet Principle

When you pray, go into your room, close the door and pray to your Father, who is unseen. Then your Father, who sees what is done in secret, will reward you.

Matthew 6:6

The kingdom of God operates very differently from the world's system. The world acknowledges the famous—even if they're famous for simply being famous.

In the kingdom of God, that which is done in secret is acknowledged. I call it "The Closet Principle." God pays attention to what is done in the secret chambers. What we do in secret is what moves us in public.

For a man's ways are in full view of the Lord, and he examines all his paths.

Proverbs 5:21

The Lord knows your innermost thoughts. He examines every one of them. Deep within man are the secret plans that God has placed on deposit there.

No eye has seen, no ear has heard, no mind has conceived what God has prepared for those who love him.

I Corinthians 2:9

God doesn't want you to replicate what you have seen. He is not interested in a verbatim recording of what you've heard, nor can your mind scheme and come up with an image of what you should do and be. God has a secret for you, hidden deep within the secluded reservoirs of your heart.

What you do in secret is what moves you in public.

Understanding "The Closet Principle" will help you draw out this secret wisdom of God. God only reveals it by His Spirit.

> *"The Spirit searches all things, even the deep things of God. For who among men knows the thoughts of a man except the man's spirit within him?" In the same way no one knows the thoughts of God except the Spirit of God.*
>
> *I Corinthians 2:10–11*

Very few men will take the time necessary to explore the deep things that God has hidden within them. They will not explore those secret arenas, choosing rather to simply imitate what they see around them.

They are content just to "keep up with the Joneses." That's even why you see most men adopt their mode of dress from their buddies.

As I travel, I have found it interesting to watch how people from different regions dress. Walking through any airport, I can usually pick out where a person is from simply by looking at the clothes they are sporting. You can also tell what type of music they like. It's usually obvious who are diehard sport fanatics because they often wear their team's colors. More subtle are the men and women is business attire. It takes a little more effort to distinguish the bankers from the attorneys. Unfortunately, preachers can also be easily spotted.

Most men simply adopt the acceptable attire and style of the norm around them. Few will step up and dress really well, representing themselves with excellence. But apart from how we dress, my point is that the way a man easily adapts his clothing to his surroundings is how he normally accepts other practices in his culture, his language, and his attitude.

Instead of just going with the flow, it is time that men hide themselves in their closets and get the wisdom of God for their lives. We need men who are willing to pay the price to distinguish themselves from the pack.

One of the surest ways to be distinguished is by drawing upon the secret place of your life. Within every person is the secret chamber that God has placed on deposit. Your uniqueness is found there. It is what is of most value not only to yourself but to the world.

"The Closet Principle" will work *for* you, or *against* you. If you spend your secret time sowing to your flesh, you will reap destruction.

> *"Are you confused about life, don't know what's going on? Steal off with me, I'll show you a good time! No one will ever know—I'll give you the time of your life." But they don't know about all the skeletons in her closet, that all her guests end up in hell.*
>
> Proverbs 9:17–18 MSG

How you spend your secret time—what you do when no one else is seeing you, determines how you reap a spiritual harvest.

Slaves, obey your earthly masters with respect and fear, and with sincerity of heart, just as you would obey Christ. Obey them not only to win their favor when their eye is on you, but like slaves of Christ, doing the will of God from your heart. Serve wholeheartedly, as if you were serving the Lord, not men, because you know that the Lord will reward everyone for whatever good he does, whether he is slave or free.

Ephesians 6:6–8

Few people recognize the enormous power that comes to those who understand "The Closet Principle." This was one of the greatest strengths of Jesus' life, He knew how to isolate Himself in order to prepare for public ministry.

For whatever is hidden is meant to be disclosed and whatever is concealed is meant to be brought out into the open.

Mark 4:22

Think about the daily rhythm of Jesus. He regularly began His day in isolation, withdrawn from the crowd and even from the disciples. Even though Jesus knew He would only serve approximately three years in public ministry, He would usually withdraw after ministering.

Jesus went on from there, two blind men followed him, calling out, "Have mercy on us, Son of David!" When he had gone indoors, the blind men came to him, and he asked them, "Do you believe that I am able to do this?" "Yes, Lord," they replied. Then he touched their eyes and said, "According to your faith will it be done to you;" and their sight was restored. Jesus warned them sternly, "See that no one knows about this." But they went out and spread the news about him all over that region.

Matthew 9:27–31

Jesus went out of His way to keep things secret. Notice, that Jesus instructed the men not to tell anyone, yet they went out immediately and began to tell their story.

The blind men could now see! How would you keep that quiet?

Nevertheless, Jesus created a pattern and a rhythm for His days.

I have seen people shipwreck their lives because they did not create a rhythm in their activities.

Early on in my ministry, I could not stop. I didn't feel that I had time to waste, so I burned the candle at both ends, so to speak. Then I noticed that my relationship with my wife was suffering. I noticed that I was tired, irritable, and becoming angry. I was no longer reading the Word of God for the sake of personal enrichment. I was only reading for sermons and messages. My prayer time was more like a business meeting, rather than an intimate conversation with God.

When I saw what was happening, I backed off and rearranged my schedule and activities. I began to get up early in the mornings to isolate myself with the Lord. I began to value reading the Word of God as a dialogue with the Lord. I began to preach messages from the overflow of my isolated experiences. I also looked at my upcoming calendar of events and cut most of them. I learned that activity is not the same as productivity.

The results were amazing. My marriage soared to new heights of enjoyment. My ministry became much more productive. I no longer was tired or irritable. Strife seemed to disappear.

In my closet time, the first thing I do is meditate on God's Word. The definition of the word *meditation* presents us with a word picture of a cow that chews on its cud. To *meditate* means to *mutter; to think something over; to explore its meaning.*

Second, I confess God's opinion over me. I speak clearly that I have accepted Jesus Christ as my Savior, that I am filled with and have fellowship with the Holy Spirit, and that the love of the Father is mine.

Third, I take authority over vain imaginations. I choose to control my thought life. I give no place for the devil in my thoughts. Whatever speaks in opposition to the Word of God is removed from my thinking.

Finally, I pray in the Holy Spirit. I ask that He will help me in my weaknesses. Sometimes, I don't know what I should be praying about, so I yield my agenda to Him. I pray, "Holy Spirit, you have much more information than I have. You know what is happening around me more than I do, so help me know how to pray."

SECTION 2
How to Be a Person of Authority

Chapter 6
Positioned by Principles

I tell this one, "Go," and he goes; and that one, "Come," and he comes. I say to my servant, "Do this," and he does it.

Matthew 9:9

The centurion's authority flowed *through* him, not *around* him. The leadership above him gave him the necessary authority to handle what was beneath him. God places you *under* authority so you can master what He has placed you *over*.

The centurion was properly positioned as a man of authority.

How do you position yourself to be a person of authority? How do you secure your spot within the protocol of authority?

To be a person of authority you must stay in alignment with the established hierarchy. If you are not completely submitted to those above you, you cannot discharge your authority to those underneath you.

If you're going to be in leadership, you must live by principles. You must control your behavior by submitting to a higher law. Doing so not only secures your proper alignment under authority, but it also ensures that you will receive the rewards which correspond to your obedience.

God places you under authority so you can master what He has placed you over.

The Principle of Honor

All the principles of God's Word have corresponding benefits. Even the restrictive commands of "thou shalt not" have positive benefits for the obedient.

The fifth command of the Ten Commandments says, "Honor your father and your mother, so that you may live long in the land the Lord your God is giving you" *(Exodus 20:12)*. This precept gives us an established rule of behavior and the corresponding reward.

In Hebrew, to *honor* means *to bear up under.* So the commandment to honor aligns the descendent within the established etiquette of authority. Obedience to the command of proper alignment promises a long and prosperous life.

This principle is reiterated by Solomon in Proverbs, "My son, do not forget my teaching, but keep my commands in your heart, for they will prolong your life many years and bring you prosperity" *(Proverbs 3:1–2)*.

Paul also emphasizes this benefit when he states in Ephesians 6:2–3, "Honor your father and mother—which is the first commandment with a promise—that it may go well with you and that you may enjoy long life on the earth."

All authority should be submitted to higher authority.

The principle is this: All authority should be submitted to higher authority.

Any leader who only has followers is a cult. Anyone who is delusional enough to think that they are the source of all knowledge, wisdom, and revelation should be avoided like the plague. A leader who does not live positioned under principles forfeits his authority.

The centurion said, "I am a man under authority, therefore I say to my servant…"

I learned very early in my walk with Christ that I had to change my behavioral patterns to conform to God's Word. I had to "study to show myself approved" *(II Timothy 2:15)*.

One day, while reading the Book of Proverbs, I ran across the verse that states, "Do not say to your neighbor, 'Come back later; I'll give it tomorrow'—when you now have it with you" *(Proverbs 3:28)*.

I kept reading because I thought, *"My neighbors don't ever ask me for anything. This is not a problem for me."* But the Holy Spirit prompted me to read that verse again. After reading it the second time, I said in my spirit, "I've got that covered." Again, the Holy Spirit said, "Look at this verse, and meditate on it. You're missing the point."

I meditated on the scripture verse searching for the principle God was trying to get me to see, until I found it. I realized that I received bills and invoices in the mail almost daily. The principle in the verse was instructing me to pay them immediately, without hesitation, to release the payment.

Now, in the natural, you might think, *"Why would you send a payment to the electric company before the bill is due? When they send the bill, you still have several days, or even a couple of weeks to pay it."*

I began to look for the corresponding benefit that obeying this principle would bring into my life. I asked the Holy Spirit to help me understand. He instructed me, "Neil, if you will pay the bill when you receive it, I will be able to release the harvests that are due to you immediately. You won't have to wait until later. The measure that you use is the same measure that I use."

You can imagine how life-changing this principle was for me. Most people have a theology on the timing of the Lord that is erroneous. They think that God arrives at the last minute, or that sometimes He is even late. Nothing could be further from the truth. The Bible teaches that, the Lamb was slain *before* the foundations of the earth. *(See Revelation 13:8.)*

God is never late—but we are. Many times we are slothfully late when it comes to our relationships. We are the ones who fail to give honor where and when it is due.

> *Give everyone what you owe him: If you owe taxes, pay taxes; if revenue,*
> *then revenue; if respect, then respect; if honor, then honor.*
>
> Romans 13:7

We must choose to live under the principles of Scripture. Doing so will bring a sure reward.

The Principle of Integrity

Another principle that the Word teaches is that we should be positioned under integrity.

> *May integrity and uprightness protect me, because my hope is in you.*
>
> Psalm 25:21

In the Hebrew, the word *integrity* is a numeric term meaning *in full measure*. It gives the idea that something is *indivisible* or *lacking corruption*. To say that a building is structurally sound a person might say, "It has integrity," meaning that there is no corruption in its components, and it is not lacking in its design.

When the centurion approached Jesus, his request showed that he had a deep understanding of how authority flows through leadership.

> *Just say the word, and my servant will be healed.*
>
> *Matthew 8:8*

The centurion realized that Jesus and His spoken word were the same. That there is no divisible difference between them. The words of Jesus are incorruptible. *(See I Peter 1:23.)*

Having recognized the integrity of Jesus, the centurion's request makes perfect sense. He knew that it wasn't necessary to have the physical presence of Jesus to have the authority of Jesus. The authority of Jesus was transferred through the command of Jesus—or through His Word.

Jesus made note that **the centurion's understanding of authority resulted in his great faith.** Jesus marveled and said, "I have not found anyone in Israel with such great faith" *(Matthew 8:10)*.

Understanding authority will give you the ability to have great faith!

Let me also say: unless you truly recognize the protocol of authority, you will not operate in biblical faith.

*I say to you that many will come from the East and the West, and will
take their places at the feast with Abraham, Isaac and Jacob in the
kingdom of heaven. But the subjects of the kingdom will be thrown
outside, into the darkness, where there will be weeping and gnashing of
teeth.*

Matthew 8:11–12

I have known many people who have professed great faith but lacked integrity toward leadership. They claim a close relationship with God yet treat their brothers with dishonor.

At the very moment when the centurion made his request his young servant was healed.

*Then Jesus said to the centurion, "Go! It will be done just as you believed
it would." And his servant was healed at that very hour.*

Matthew 8:13

Notice too that Jesus practiced the principle of Proverbs 3:28. He did not say to the centurion, "Well, why don't you come back tomorrow?" No, Jesus spoke His Word at that very moment. His Word of integrity was released and fulfilled within the hour.

I am watching to see that my word is fulfilled.

Jeremiah 1:12

God watches over His Word. It is imperative that He does. All of creation—the Earth, the universe—everything relies upon the integrity of God's Word. He cannot allow one word to go unheeded.

God is not flippant in his communication. He isn't casual in His language. He is very prudent and very precise when He speaks. God doesn't toy with us. He isn't prone to jesting or demeaning language.

> *God is not a man, that he should lie, nor a son of man, that he should change his mind. Does he speak and then not act? Does he promise and not fulfill?*
>
> *Genesis 23:19*

We're living in a time when people are very loose in their conversations. Our politicians embellish their resumés while they campaign. That is becoming very dangerous, since everything that they say can be authenticated or proven false with a few keystrokes and a Google search. When Hillary Clinton "misspoke" on several occasions about her trip to Bosnia, she was discovered within minutes. When Barack Obama suggested his uncle helped liberate Auschwitz, it was revealed that the only way that his uncle could have done so is if he served in the Red Army of Russia, for it was the Russians who liberated Auschwitz.

These examples demonstrate how the public has loosened its standard of defining what is a lie and what is really the truth. In today's world, a "lie" to me might not be a "lie" to you. According to former President Bill Clinton, it would all depend on what *your definition* of the word *lie* is.

If you fabricate your resumé to obtain a job in the corporate world, or if you embellish your credentials to become a professor at a university, you will be fired for committing a fraudulent act. Yet, to become the leader of the free world, you can simply "misspeak." *(Please excuse my sarcasm.)*

To follow the protocol of authority, we must commit ourselves to live by the principle of integrity.

Chapter 7

Watch Over Your Words

To be a person of authority you must watch over your words.

My daughter, Courtney came to me one day and said, "Dad, I need a new Blackberry cell phone."

I answered, "No, honey, you don't *need* a new cell phone. You *want* a new cell phone." Then I explained the difference between needs and desires.

She adjusted her petition and said, "Daddy, I know that you're a good and loving father who delights in granting the desires of my heart. I would like to have a new Blackberry cell phone." *(She wasn't flattering me, she was practicing proper protocol.)*

Her request was aimed at getting me to say something. She wanted me to say, "Yes" or "I promise." Once I affirm her request, she no longer asks me.

Then she moves to the next stage of her request. She begins to remind me of what I said. Until I get her the phone, she comes back to me and says, "Dad, you said…"

What is she doing?

She is returning my words to me, knowing that I must agree with myself.

So is my word that goes out from my mouth: It will not return to me empty, but will accomplish what I desire and achieve the purpose for which I sent it.

Isaiah 55:11

When we speak words, we align our behavior to our promises. That's why it is extremely important to watch over what we say.

As a person of authority, you must have confidence in what you say. If you don't trust your own words, you can't pray in faith.

There are two types of words that should never be used. The first is *cussing*, and the second is *cursing*. *Cussing* is ignorantly using expletives when you lack the vocabulary to express yourself. It's a lazy person's expression. Many of today's song writers, comedians, and actors are prone to launching these projectile words out of their foolish minds. They lack the creativity to say what they want to say without letting vileness pour out of their mouths.

When a person of authority yells profanity to intimidate a subservient, it lowers him and his office. Don't use profanity, it makes you look like an imbecile.

Cursing is when people invoke poverty, sickness, disaster, destruction, or death upon themselves or others, saying things like, "That's driving me crazy," "You're killing me," or "That blows my mind."

I'm amazed at how frivolous people are with the words that come out of their mouths. I hear people who would never use profanity, speak curses without restraint.

I had a family member who used to say, "I don't know what's wrong with me—I must have a tumor on the brain!" She said it for years. Since she has had three tumors removed from her brain, we've suggested that she should no longer say that.

Words are powerful. God will not release more power into your life, if He can't trust you with your words. You will never have a full measure of authority, until you have integrity with your words.

Gossip and Slander

> *I tell you that men will have to give account on the day of judgment for every careless word they have spoken. For by your words you will be acquitted, and by your words you will be condemned.*
>
> *Matthew 12:36–37*

Another failure that hinders the flow of authority in our lives is the insatiable appetite that we have for gossip and slander. The Apostle Paul says that a person who speaks gossip or slander has a depraved mind. *(See Romans 1:28.)* Depravity is the antithesis of integrity.

The word *gossip* literally means *to whisper secret chants to charm snakes.* Gossip is a form of witchcraft. Gossips are whisperers. They hide in corners of the room. They have crafty eyes, darting to and fro. They plant suspicions in the minds of others.

To slander means *to speak evil or to defame.* Slander is the attempt to kill another person's reputation.

Let me give a biblical illustration about how powerfully deceptive slander is.

Jonathan son of Saul had a son who was lame in both feet. He was five years old when the news about Saul and Jonathan came from Jezreel. His nurse picked him up and fled, but as she hurried to leave, he fell and became crippled. His name was Mephibosheth.

II Samuel 4:4

When he came to power, King David wanted to honor and be kind to someone in the household of Saul because of his dear friend Jonathan. A servant named Ziba came forward with information concerning Mephibosheth. David called for Mephibosheth to enter into his favor. Every day he was to eat at the King's table. He also inherited the entire estate of Saul, his grandfather.

Years later, David had to flee because of a rebellion instigated by his own son, Absalom. While David was exiting the city, Ziba showed up with supplies for David and his entire army.

The king asked Ziba, "Why have you brought these?"

Ziba answered, "The donkeys are for the king's household to ride on, the bread and fruit are for the men to eat, and the wine is to refresh those who become exhausted in the desert."

The king then asked, "Where is your master's grandson?'

Ziba said to him, "He is staying in Jerusalem, because he thinks, 'Today the house of Israel will give me back my grandfather's kingdom.'"

Then the king said to Ziba, "All that belonged to Mephibosheth is now yours."

"I humbly bow," Ziba said. "May I find favor in your eyes, my lord the king."

II Samuel 16:1–4

Ziba had schemed against his master, Mephibosheth. He worked hard to endear himself to the King. His wickedness was apparent as he despised the handicap of his boss.

When David returned to the city, Mephibosheth came out to meet him.

Mephibosheth, Saul's grandson, also went down to meet the king. He had not taken care of his feet or trimmed his mustache or washed his clothes from the day the king left until the day he returned safely.

When he came from Jerusalem to meet the king, the king asked him, "Why didn't you go with me, Mephibosheth?"

He said, "My lord the king, since I your servant am lame, I said, 'I will have my donkey saddled and will ride on it, so I can go with the king.' But Ziba my servant betrayed me. And he has slandered your servant to my lord the king. My lord the king is like an angel of God; so do whatever pleases you. All my grandfather's descendants deserved nothing but death from my lord the king, but you gave your servant a place among those who eat at your table. So what right do I have to make any more appeals to the king?"

II Samuel 19:24–28

Look at how powerful slander can be. Even though Ziba lied about Mephibosheth, David did not discern Ziba's deceptive scheme. As a result, David divided what rightfully belonged to

Mephibosheth between him and Ziba. Mephibosheth proved his loyalty and said, "Let him have it all, that's not what is important to me" *(II Samuel 19:30).*

Once slander defiles a person, it is very difficult to regain honor. A question usually hangs over him for years—or sometimes even for his entire life.

Slanderous language is considered so vile that the Old Testament judgment pronounced for the crimes of slander and gossip was capital punishment.

> *They have become filled with every kind of wickedness, evil, greed and depravity. They are full of envy, murder, strife, deceit and malice. They are gossips, slanderers, God-haters, insolent, arrogant and boastful; they invent ways of doing evil; they disobey their parents; they are senseless, faithless, heartless, ruthless. Although they know God's righteous decree that those who do such things deserve death, they not only continue to do these very things but also approve of those who practice them.*
>
> *Romans 1:29–32*

In God's eyes, the verbal assassination of a person's character is akin to murder. If you think that I am being hard on this subject, look at what Solomon said: "The tongue has the power of life and death, and those who love it will eat its fruit" *(Proverbs 18:21).*

Jesus chose His Words carefully. He said, "I did not speak of my own accord, but the Father who sent me commanded me what to say and how to say it" *(John 12:49).*

Jesus confined His words to what His Father said. *(See John 14:10.)* He also demonstrated the protocol of authority in how He said it.

I know that his command leads to eternal life. So whatever I say is just what the Father has told me to say.

John 12:50

I travel each week speaking in churches, teaching seminars, and conducting Fivestar Man Encounters. I can't estimate how many times I have prayed for grown men and women who are still controlled by the loose words that a person of authority spoke over them when they were a child.

Not long ago, while ministering in a church, I felt the Holy Spirit prompt me to pray for a couple. I asked them to come forward and asked permission to pray for them. They agreed.

As I laid my hands upon their foreheads while praying, my mind began to see scenes of the woman's childhood. She was thirteen years old, she was joyfully dancing around in her bedroom, laughing and playing, when her father came by the room and began to speak harsh and angry words over her. He bruised her spirit. It was that moment—that very instance—that caused her to withdraw into a cocoon spiritually and emotionally. She began to accept that a father was mean, controlling, harsh, and angry.

When I described the scene that played out in my mind, the woman uncontrollably burst into tears. Sobbing and wrenching before me, she allowed the pent-up emotion of decades to come forth.

I then turned to her husband, and spoke a word over him. "Without knowing that this occurred in her young life, you have also used harsh words and outbursts of rage to control your wife." He confessed to me that he didn't know why he had done this and that it was out of his normal character to do so, but he admitted that he did speak to his wife this way to get what he wanted.

That couple was delivered from that horrific pattern in their marriage that day. The husband pledged to never again use harsh, angry words to control his wife. She released her father in forgiveness, and she committed not to allow that moment from so many years ago to control her life from that day on.

Chapter 8
Fulfill Your Vows

Making a vow is a verbal commitment to consecrate oneself to a course of action or purpose, or to voluntarily dedicate a gift or offering. To *vow* literally conveys the idea of *falling down, prostrating oneself as wheat on the threshing floor.*

We live in a society that thinks nothing of making vain promises. We see it in the nonchalant attitude toward marriage. The debate rages concerning the sanctity of marriage: What constitutes a marriage? Whom can a person marry? How many people can be in a marriage? How long should a marriage last? The sanctity of the marriage vows has been reduced to prenuptial promises that have a life span as long as goose bumps on the arm. Society as a whole has turned marriage into nothing more than a drunken fling in Vegas, lasting all of fifteen minutes.

When we stand at an altar and speak words that commit our lives to one another with God as our witness, it is a very serious matter.

As a pastor, I have counseled many young couples concerning this issue. I can say without exaggeration that most of them had the idea that marriage was just a step beyond "going steady." Their commitment level was elementary. I promised myself that I would not participate as a minister in marriages that were approached with insincerity.

> *When you make a vow to God, do not delay in fulfilling it. He has no pleasure in fools; fulfill your vow. It is better not to vow than to make a vow and not fulfill it. Do not let your mouth lead you into sin. And do not*

> *protest to the temple messenger, "My vow was a mistake." Why should*
> *God be angry at what you say and destroy the work of your hands?*
>
> Ecclesiastes 5:4–6

As people of authority, we must be very diligent in committing ourselves and making vows. There is a direct correlation between fulfilling our vows and success in our work.

Have you ever worked at something tirelessly yet had no results? Does it seem as if everything works against you?

Examine your words. Have you promised something that you have been slack in keeping? Have you brushed off a commitment? What have you promised that you need to immediately fulfill?

> *If you have been trapped by what you said, ensnared by the words of your*
> *mouth, then do this, my son, to free yourself, since you have fallen into*
> *your neighbor's hands: Go and humble yourself; press your plea with*
> *your neighbor! Allow no sleep to your eyes, no slumber to your eyelids.*
> *Free yourself, like a gazelle from the hand of the hunter, like a bird from*
> *the snare of the fowler.*
>
> Proverbs 6:2–5

Do you see the intensity in the effort to get free? Solomon says, "You're trapped by your words!"

Have you ever seen a trapped animal? When an animal gets caged it goes wild. It scraps and claws at everything. There is nothing more dangerous than a trapped animal. This is the first stage of being trapped. But then something else happens.

Have you ever seen an animal that has been caged for a long time? It loses hope. It cowers and mopes around. Its eyes are glazed over, its health wanes, and its spirit is extinguished.

When people have rashly committed themselves for long periods of time, they take on the nature of an animal which has been trapped for a long time. You can see the hopelessness in the faces of people who are bound by debt. People who choose to entangle themselves with credit cards and excessive debt never can see a way out.

Making any vow—whether it regards finances or something else—is a very serious matter.

The Bible gives us a sobering example of a man who committed to a vow rashly and produced a horrendous result.

Not unlike the situation in Israel today, God's people were facing a war over the land God had promised to give them. Israel was facing hostilities with its neighbors. God's people needed a warrior—a leader who could stand up against their rivals. They needed a courageous, rough type of a man, who was willing and able to fight.

> *The leaders of the people of Gilead said to each other, "Whoever will launch the attack against the Ammonites will be the head of all those living in Gilead."*
>
> *Judges 10:18*

The Israelites needed a strong leader. They needed Jephthah.

Jephthah was the son of a Gileadite and a prostitute. Because of his illegitimate conception, his brothers despised and rejected him. They disinherited him and drove him out of their lives, but the tables had turned, and they needed him to deliver them.

Jephthah was a man's man. He was a mighty warrior who surrounded himself with other adventurers who were loyal to him. He was conditioned for the field of contest.

After negotiations with the elders, Jephthah agreed to return to his own people and to become their leader. The Ammonites were an incestuous people, the descendants of vile relations. Jephthah sent evidence to them of the rightful ownership of the land through his messengers; however, the King of Ammon dismissed the message.

The Spirit of the Lord came upon Jephthah, preparing him for battle. It was at this point that Jephthah made an immature and fatal declaration.

> *And Jephthah made a vow to the Lord: "If you give the Ammonites into my hands, whatever comes out of the door of my house to meet me when I return in triumph from the Ammonites will be the Lord's and I will sacrifice it as a burnt offering."*
>
> *Judges 11:30–31*

Never make a flippant vow while you are filled with spiritual excitement. Many people who get near the presence of God make hasty promises, commitments, or vows which they are unable or unwilling to keep.

> *Guard your steps when you go to the house of God. Go near to listen rather than to offer the sacrifice of fools, who do not know that they do wrong. Do not be quick with your mouth, do not be hasty in your heart to utter anything before God. God is in heaven and you are on earth, so let your words be few.*
>
> *Ecclesiastes 5:1–2*

One of the services that my ministry provides is consulting churches and organizations on financial campaigns. I encourage leaders to cast the vision of the project and give people faith to follow that vision to completion. *(For more information on this topic, see my book entitled, The Seven Laws Which Govern Increase and Order.)*

Unfortunately, I have seen so-called "professional stewardship services" use manipulative and ungodly strategies to try to raise funds from God's people. It is not only ineffective, it is sinful.

We should be very diligent in the way that we approach the offering. When we ask people to financially pledge or vow to the Lord, we should do it with sober reflection. We should encourage people to examine their hearts on the matter.

I've attended services where professional representatives use highly-charged, emotional appeals to manipulate finances from people. It leaves a distaste in my gut. When people leave the services, they have "giver's remorse." They feel used, thinking, *"They got to me again!"*

> *Each man should give what he has decided in his heart to give, not*
> *reluctantly or under compulsion, for God loves a cheerful giver.*
> II Corinthians 9:7

The word *compulsion* in this verse literally *means folding the arm*. It conveys the thought that the gift is only being released by forceful extraction. The image is like a merchant being forced to payoff the mob boss with "protection" money in order to operate his business safely. Unfortunately, many fundraising tactics represent God that way. They compel people to give out of fear of reprisal or to secure divine protection.

Jephthah made such a vow. It had catastrophic consequences.

> *When Jephthah returned to his home in Mizpah, who should come out to meet him but his daughter, dancing to the sound of tambourines! She was an only child. Except for her he had neither son nor daughter. When he saw her, he tore his clothes and cried, "Oh! My daughter! You have made me miserable and wretched, because I have made a vow to the Lord that I cannot break."*
>
> *Judges 11:34–35*

I can't imagine anything more tragic than this moment. Make no mistake about it, God was not pleased with this. God did not ask for his daughter to be sacrificed, nor has He ever been pleased with such offerings. The one and only time that God asked that a person be sacrificed was when He intervened with His own provision and fulfilled His own request. *(See Genesis 22.)*

The point that we must remember is that making a vow with our lips is a very sober and serious thing.

If we are going to become people of authority, we must watch over our words and keep our promises. Our words are full of authority and they carry the power of life and death within them.

Chapter 9

Influence Brings Authority

Influence is a form of currency. In fact, influence has a better rate of exchange than silver or gold.

> *A good name is more desirable than great riches; to be esteemed is better than silver or gold.*
>
> Proverbs 22:1

Cornelius, a centurion living in Caesarea, was a man of influence. He came from one of the most prominent families in all of Rome. Generations of his predecessors served in high ranks of leadership.

> *At Caesarea there was a man named Cornelius, a centurion in what was known as the Italian Regiment. He and all his family were devout and God-fearing; he gave generously to those in need and prayed to God regularly.*
>
> Acts 10:1–2

What distinguished Cornelius was his spirituality. He was noble and reverent in respect toward God. His devotion became influential to God and man. (*For further study on the Currency of Influence, see my book, God's Currency.*)

One day, at 3 p.m., an angel called Cornelius by name.

Cornelius, always respectful toward authority responded, "What is it, Lord?"

Remember, the term "Lord" is a term of honor denoting complete supremacy. Cornelius showed reverential respect toward the angelic visitor and toward God.

The angel answered Cornelius, "Your prayers and gifts to the poor have come up as a memorial offering before God."

A *memorial offering* is an offering which causes a perpetual memory. In the Old Testament, a memorial offering was offered in conjunction with the burning of frankincense so that it would be a fragrant reminder to the Lord. Cornelius' gifts served as an aroma of remembrance to the Lord.

All miracles are worked through people.

God was about to do a tremendous miracle for the Gentile world, but all miracles are worked through people. The Lord wanted Cornelius and Peter to meet, so He told Cornelius to send servants to Joppa, where Peter was staying with Simon, the tanner.

God always works through relationships. That's why networking with people is so vital to your life.

To confirm the arrangements, God also gave Peter a vision at noon the following day. Peter was waiting on the roof of the house for lunch to be served when he suddenly fell into a trance. The vision addressed a theological breakthrough Christ had brought to the dietary laws of the Jews. The Gospel of Christ cleansed all food for consumption. God used the example of sanctification of food to teach Peter that the Gentiles were also acceptable to God through the Gospel. To the Jew, this was a radical concept.

After Peter had seen this vision three times, the servants of Cornelius arrived at the house where Peter was staying.

We have come from Cornelius the centurion. He is a righteous and God-fearing man, who is respected by all the Jewish people. A holy angel told him to have you come to his house so that he could hear what you have to say.

Acts 10:22

The servants who approached Peter argued that Cornelius' life testified of righteous, God-fearing, honor. Think about how influential this man was that God would send angels to carry a message about him, and his servants would speak up on his behalf.

Much like the centurion who approached Jesus, the issue that arose for Peter was the appropriateness of entering the house of a Gentile. Without the vision from God, Peter would have never set foot in the house, but because of the Lord's intervention, he entered the dwelling of Cornelius and shared the Gospel with Cornelius, his relatives, and the close friends he had invited into his home.

While Peter was speaking, the Holy Spirit came upon all who were there. The evidence of God's presence was marked by the Gentiles speaking in spiritual languages (other tongues) and praising God. This physical evidence confirmed to the Jews that the Gentiles were indeed accepted into the Gospel of Christ. Without this evidence, we could only have speculated that we were accepted, but because of it, we now have God's written testimony as proof.

Influence is a currency. To be people of authority we must value our influence. We must recognize the extreme worth of our names.

A name represents the person. It is common to look into the etymology of a name to understand a person's character traits. That is also why God made it a habit to change a person's name when he wanted to change their destiny.

When I was six years of age, my stepfather persuaded my mother to change my name. They no longer called me by my first name, which is Gary, my father's name. They also no longer called be by my surname which is Kennedy. I grew up under an assumed name, Neil Roberson.

At the beginning of every school year my teachers would look on their records and call out my name, "Gary Kennedy." When they did, embarrassed, I had to go up to their desks and explain the stupidity of my life.

When I became an adult, I went through the process of renewing all of my records and changed my name back to Gary Neil Kennedy.

When I did, a sense of identity came back to me. I sensed a confidence of who I was. It empowered me.

Jesus taught that His name has influence. The authority of Jesus is administered through His name.

> *I will do whatever you ask in my name, so that the Son may bring glory*
> *to the Father. You may ask me for anything in my name, and I will do it.*
> *John 14:13*

Jesus' name has tremendous influence with the Heavenly Father. There is no other name by which men can be saved, healed, delivered, or made whole.

> *My Father will give you whatever you ask in my name. Until now you*
> *have not asked for anything in my name. Ask and you will receive, and*
> *your joy will be complete.*
> *John 16:23–24*

If we are going to become people of authority, we must have a name that speaks of righteousness and God-fearing respect.

God looks for people of influence to work with. That is why it is vital that we connect with others in the marketplace and the community. We should be leaders representing God as ambassadors for Him.

SECTION 3
The Gate of Authority

Chapter 10
The Gate of Authority

> *I tell you the truth, the man who does not enter the sheep pen by the gate,
> but climbs in by some other way, is a thief and a robber. The man who
> enters by the gate is the shepherd of his sheep. The watchman opens the
> gate for him, and the sheep listen to his voice. He calls his own sheep by
> name and leads them out. When he has brought out all his own, he goes
> on ahead of them, and his sheep follow him because they know his voice.
> But they will never follow a stranger; in fact, they will run away from him
> because they do not recognize a stranger's voice.*
>
>

John 10:1–6

Jesus explained how his relationship with us is like the relationship of a shepherd and his sheep. The shepherd carries authority through his voice. The sheep know and recognize the shepherd's voice, and the shepherd knows each of his sheep by name.

I call this the Gate of Authority. Jesus teaches that in this relationship he has authority. *(See John 10:18.)*

> *I am the way and the truth and the life. No one comes to the Father
> except through me.*
>
>

John 14:6

Jesus is the only Gateway of Authority to the Father. No one can circumvent this protocol. No other name gives us access to and relationship with the Father God.

Just as Jesus is the Gate of Authority to the Father, likewise, Jesus is also the Gate of Authority from the Father to us. The Father God honors the protocol of authority that He set in place.

Jesus is the only Gate of Authority to the Father.

God will not have a relationship with you outside of His Son Jesus. This serves as a protection for you and I, because it provides separation between the physical and spiritual realms.

It is evident throughout scripture that a spirit must have access to a body to operate in the physical realm. Evil spiritual influences roam throughout the Earth, continually looking for bodies to inhabit. By establishing the protocol of authority, the Father God has provided a built-in protection for the believer. The Lord Jesus Christ is the Guard of the gateway to our spirits.

One day, I went into a tire store where I had bought a set of high-quality tires for my SUV. When I approached the counter, the manager asked if he could assist me, and I replied, "Sure, I have a flat that needs to be fixed."

I lived in a community that had a lot of construction going on in it, and I seemed to pick up quite a few nails.

As we walked out to my vehicle, I told the service manager, "You know, I bought these new tires three months ago, and I've had three flats since—"

The manager interrupted me mid-sentence. "What are you saying? Do you think that something is wrong with my tires?" The anger in his eyes was like fire, and his voice quivered with emotion in a threatening tone.

To be honest, I was so surprised by his attitude that I didn't know how to respond. I said, "Wait a minute. I wasn't finished. I was going to tell you about all the construction in my neighborhood. And by the way," I said, "these aren't your tires—they're mine. I'll just get someone else to fix them." Then I left.

As I reflected a while upon his uncontrollable anger, I was concerned enough to call his district manager. After explaining the ordeal, the district manager said, "I can't imagine why he did that. He is a very *religious* man."

The episode bothered me enough that I felt I needed an explanation for what had happened, so I prayed about the matter. The Holy Spirit revealed to me that the man certainly was a "religious" man, but he worshipped Christian images and idols. He was deceived. His relationship with God was not through Jesus Christ, but it was through deceased saints and religious rituals. The Lord revealed to me that the man had accepted familiar spirits into his own spirit. Because his heart did not harmonize with the Spirit of God within me, he had become very agitated by my presence.

Many people have replaced Jesus, the true Gate of Authority to the Father God, with false images and idols. They may believe that they are Christians, but they are not. They trade the grace and mercy of God for rituals and traditions.

> *Those who cling to worthless idols forfeit the grace that could be theirs.*
> *Jonah 2:8*

Chapter 11
Authority in the Home

In the Garden of Eden, Satan had to enter a physical body to operate on the Earth. He chose the body of a serpent. The snake began to speak with Eve, and because she was deceived, Eve listened and entertained the questions that the devil proposed. Because Eve opened herself up to a foreign source of reasoning, she began to agree with the words which perverted the Word of God. The all-consuming question within her became, "Did God *really* say…?"

When Eve turned to her husband, she repeated what she had heard, rather than return Adam's words to him. Then Adam sinned—not by being deceived—but by choosing disobedience. Adam knew what he was doing!

When God created man, He gave him *dominion,* which includes the authority "to rule, or to tread over *all creatures that move along the ground*" *(Genesis 1:26.)*. Of course, a snake is a creature that moves along the ground.

At the dawn of humanity, God established Adam as the Gate of Authority. It was through Adam that sin entered into the genetic code of mankind.

> *Sin entered the world through one man, and death through sin, and in this way death came to all men, because all sinned.*
>
> Romans 5:12

As the Gate of Authority, Adam should have resisted the snake by commanding him to depart, or by crushing his head. *(See Genesis 3:15.)* Adam should have prevented the devil from speaking to his wife.

The serpent was a law breaker. He circumvented the relationship of Adam toward Eve. He spoke *directly* to Eve. He operated outside of protocol.

Years ago, I had a neighbor who raised his voice to my wife once. He was drunk and out of control, but I was out of town at the time. When I returned, I waited for the opportunity to confront him.

Sure enough, one day in a drunken stupor, he yelled at me. When he did, I turned and approached him. Without raising my voice, I calmly addressed him by name (Proverbs 15:1). As I was drawing closer to him, he bolted toward me thinking that he could intimidate me and cause me to back down. Instead, I took two more steps *toward* him. He realized that his bullying tactics weren't going to work on me, and he stopped abruptly.

Then I looked straight into his eyes and said, "Don't raise your voice to me. You're drunk. And don't ever speak to my wife or children again. If you have something to say, be a man and come to me."

He timidly walked away. After that day, any time that I would walk out of the house, he would scurry into his garage or home with his head bowed in shame. I have dealt with that kind of spirit before. I have learned that you cannot conquer it with fear.

To be a man of authority, you must protect your home from outside forces.

Husband, you are the Gate of Authority for your wife. You should not allow just anyone to speak into her life or into the lives of your children. You cannot cower or be weak in this regard. To be a man of authority, you must protect your home from outside forces.

For the husband is the head of the wife as Christ is the head of the church, his body, of which he is the Savior. Now as the church submits to Christ, so also wives should submit to their husbands in everything.
Ephesians 5:23–24

Remember this: the head always determines the direction of the body.

Growing up, wrestling was my sport of choice. Although I played football, I wasn't very good at it because of my physical size. I was also too short for basketball. Wrestling fit me well because I could compete with someone else of my own size and weight. One thing I learned very quickly in wrestling is that if you wanted to move your opponent, you had to control his head. As goes the head—so goes the body.

The head always determines the direction of the body.

Very few men realize how significant their role as a husband plays in the lives of their wife and children.

I didn't grow up in church, so when I came to Christ, I realized that I had to change my way of thinking. I understood that my ways of doing things were insufficient. They were ways that I learned from those who went before me—my family members, teachers, coaches, etc. But none of those individuals had proven success. Failures in marriage were rampant in my family. I knew that if I was going to experience life differently, I had to find new ways of doing things.

It is insanity to do the same thing over and over with the expectation of a different outcome. I wanted a different life than what I had witnessed. So I turned to the Word of God for guidance. I decided that I would not date until I knew how to treat a lady. I refrained from dating for one complete year.

I remember the day that I found God's instructions for husbands written in Ephesians 5.

> *Husbands, love your wives, just as Christ loved the church and gave himself up for her to make her holy, cleansing her by the washing with water through the word, and to present her to himself as a radiant church, without stain or wrinkle or any other blemish, but holy and blameless. In this same way, husbands ought to love their wives as their own bodies. He who loves his wife loves himself.*
> Ephesians 5:25–28

The moment I read it, I understood how I was to treat a woman. I wanted to treat my wife the way I had always wanted my mother to be treated.

Husbands are commanded to love their wives with a sacrificial love—the kind of love that lays down its own rights and privileges on behalf of the woman. This kind of love reflects that the husband is being well pleased with and content with the wife. He is not only fond of her, but he is also completely entertained by her. So many men today forfeit their relationships with their wives because they find other women more entertaining. They don't enjoy being in their wives' company, and they are always casting their eyes onto other women.

The scripture says that Jesus gave Himself for the Church to make her holy. Just as Christ presented Himself as a sacrifice on behalf of the Church, a husband is to sacrifice himself to protect the purity and sacredness of his wife.

Ever since Genesis 3:15, there has been an enmity between the woman and the devil. Satan hates women. He knows that woman is the incubator of the seed. It was through a woman that the Seed —the Messiah—came into the world. A woman served as the channel through which the Word of God was conceived and delivered from the spirit into flesh. Therefore, Satan has attacked women from the beginning.

The world's system is never satisfied with women. Every television commercial tears down their appearance. They're never good enough. They are never smart enough. They can't reduce their body weight enough to ever satisfy the insatiable appetite of ungodly judgment. In the world, women can never measure up.

The world's system is never satisfied with women.

A husband should serve as the Gate of Authority for his wife. He should never allow his wife to be compared with the unhealthy image that the world holds as beauty. He must speak encouraging and reassuring words to build her up and strengthen her character.

> *... cleansing her by the washing with water through the word.*
>
> *Ephesians 5:26*

The husband's words are to be a cleansing agent for his wife. The words he speaks with his authority should literally sanctify her spirit. A husband's words go deep into a wife's soul and will reflect upon her appearance. The wife is a reflection of her husband's care for her.

He must present her to himself as a radiant bride *(Ephesians 5:27)*. To be *radiant* means *to be notable, glorious, illustrious, and esteemed.* It also denotes the idea of *splendid in clothing.* The husband should look to adorn his wife properly. He must take care that she is able to present herself as esteemed in her appearance.

Ephesians 5:27 speaks of the wholesomeness that come from the husband's delicate care for his wife. As he nurtures her, he provides himself with a wife "without stain or wrinkle or any other blemish, but holy and blameless" in her conduct. The husband's tender care and gentle words are what keep his wife pure and faithful in her marriage relationship with him.

God instructed Abraham to change his wife's name from Sarai, meaning *princess,* to *Sarah,* which means *noble woman.* Why would God want Abraham to change her name?

Because, as her husband, Abraham had the authority to cleanse her and sanctify her by the washing of his words. Calling her Sarah, Noble Woman, was a maturing process for her. She was no longer just a princess. She was to be considered a queen.

This apparently had a great affect upon her beauty for she was so attractive that more than one king desired to have her as his own. *(See Genesis 12:10–20; 20:1–18.)*

According to the Word of God, the wife is the husband's own flesh *(Ephesians 5:28)*. Whatever she looks like is really a sign of what he looks like.

This is a great lesson for men to receive. Instead of Abraham desiring a younger woman and trying to keep his wife a princess, by speaking over her that she was a noble woman, he taught her how to mature and how to become elegant in her age.

There is nothing more disheartening and sad than to see an older woman trying to imitate a teenager in clothing, makeup, and a hairstyle that looks too young for her. In truth, it's a poor commentary on her husband.

I want my wife to mature gracefully. I want to build her up with my words, to strengthen her with my confidence.

Chapter 12
Don't Be Weak-Kneed

Strengthen your feeble arms and weak knees.

Hebrews 12:12

When things are difficult and times are hard, a husband must draw his strength from his personal relationship with God, and then he must turn and strengthen his wife. Don't be weak-kneed when it comes to challenge and crisis.

Husband, your wife is not your mother! Stand up and be a man. Don't try to draw your strength from your wife. You should be the one to give her strength. Your steadfast resolve in the face of crisis will give her unwavering confidence.

I've seen guys who constantly poor-mouth to their wives, or they whine about all their troubles. They show incredible weakness, and some even sob and cry like little babies in front of their wives.

A great illustration of this kind of anemic guy is found in the story of Ahab. Ahab goes down in the books as one of the most wicked kings in Israel's history. He married the infamous Jezebel, who was the epitome of a woman without authority.

There was never a man like Ahab, who sold himself to do evil in the eyes of the Lord, urged on by Jezebel his wife. He behaved in the vilest manner by going after idols, like the Amorites the Lord drove out before Israel.

I Kings 21:25–26

You know the story. Ahab set his eyes upon a neighbor's vineyard. He coveted Naboth's property.

> But Naboth replied, "The Lord forbid that I should give you the inheritance of my fathers."
>
> So Ahab went home, sullen and angry because Naboth the Jezreelite had said, "I will not give you the inheritance of my fathers." He lay on his bed sulking and refused to eat.
>
> His wife Jezebel came in and asked him, "Why are you so sullen? Why won't you eat?"
>
> He answered her, "Because I said to Naboth the Jezreelite, 'Sell me your vineyard; or if you prefer, I will give you another vineyard in its place.' But he said, 'I will not give you my vineyard.'"
>
> Jezebel his wife said, "Is this how you act as king over Israel? Get up and eat! Cheer up. I'll get you the vineyard of Naboth the Jezreelite."
>
> I Kings 21:3–7

Ahab was a weak man and a whiner. Jezebel took his stationery, his seal, and his signature and wrote letters that revealed how truly wicked she was. The plot involved pronouncing a fast, slandering an innocent man, and murdering that man to seize his property.

Ahab was the Gate of Authority—for his wife and for the nation of Israel. Because he failed to lead his wife and his people, God's prophet released a curse upon all of Ahab's family. Ahab's progeny would be cut off forever.

Strong women require very strong men to give them proper leadership.

Ahab married a woman who's name meant "without cohabitation." Although married, Jezebel was an independent woman. She married Ahab, but she never submitted to his leadership. She refused to be led by his weak, emotive authority.

I admire strong women, but they require very strong men to give them proper leadership.

As a pastor, I have had many situations that have arisen within the church that required my attention. I can honestly say that most of them involved couples that did not have a proper protocol of authority in their homes. Most of the men involved were weak. Their feeble attempts to lead their strong-willed wives were disastrous. Often when one of these couples came to speak with me, the wife would expect that I would react in a similar fashion as her husband. Usually, to her surprise, I didn't. I knew then that it wouldn't be long before the couple would leave my church unable to submit to authority.

When my wife and I got married, I was weak in leadership ability. I didn't believe that I had the moral authority to lead her. She was raised in church and had lived a very pure and holy lifestyle. I was raised a heathen and lived in sin until I got saved. It took me a couple of years to see how important it was for me to step up and give her leadership as a husband even though I sometimes felt awkward.

Chapter 13
Don't Be a Foolish Man

> *David moved down into the Desert of Maon. A certain man in Maon,*
> *who had property there at Carmel, was very wealthy. He had a thousand*
> *goats and three thousand sheep, which he was shearing in Carmel. His*
> *name was Nabal and his wife's name was Abigail. She was an intelligent*
> *and beautiful woman, but her husband, a Calebite, was surly and mean*
> *in his dealings.*
>
> > *I Samuel 25:1–3*

Some women receive their strength from integrity, even though their husbands may act like fools.

David heard that Nabal was shearing sheep, which was normally a time marked by a celebration of sorts. It was customarily a time when people showed generosity and gratitude. David heard of the festivities and sent messengers to ask for supplies. Nabal response was dismissive and demeaning.

> *Nabal answered David's servants, "Who is this David? Who is this son of*
> *Jesse? Many servants are breaking away from their masters these days.*
> *Why should I take my bread and water, and the meat I have slaughtered*
> *for my shearers, and give it to men coming from who knows where?"*
>
> > *I Samuel 25:10–11*

When he received this news, David and 400 of his 600 men put on their swords. As they broke toward Nabal's property they were stopped by a woman. Nabal's wife, Abigail, was told by a servant how her husband had responded to David's request. Knowing that her husband was ruthless and mean, she attempted to stop the confrontation.

Abigail offered gifts of two hundred loaves of bread, two skins of wine, five dressed sheep, a bushel of roasted grain, a hundred cakes of raisins and two hundred cakes of figs to appease David's righteous anger. She fell down at his feet and explained that she had not seen his servants or heard their requests. She begged David to forgive the foolishness of her husband, Nabal, for his name literally meant "fool."

David acknowledged Abigail's good judgment and blessed her.

When Abigail returned to her husband, he was holding a banquet like a king. True to his character, he was drunk. Abigail waited until he sobered up to tell him what she had done to save his life. When she did, he immediately suffered a heart attack. He died ten days later.

The lips of the righteous nourish many, but fools die for lack of judgment.
Proverbs 10:21

Abigail's actions nourished David's men, while Nabal's lack of judgment killed him.

A man's strength doesn't come from financial success. Nabal was very financially successful but he was a fool. Don't be a weak or foolish man. Step up and be strong. A man's strength comes from good judgment and wisdom.

So many men mistakenly evaluate their worth by their wallets. They have a narcissistic view of themselves because of their achievements.

Solomon taught that this kind of thinking is vanity.

*Better a poor but wise youth than an old but foolish king who no longer
knows how to take warning.*

Ecclesiastes 4:13

Pay attention to this warning. We've all seen men who work diligently in their youth to acquire the reward of wealth, and then at middle-age they begin to question their worth. They face a "half-time" crisis. Rather than reevaluating the course that they are on, they act foolishly, like an adolescent wanting to go to the high school prom again.

I remember as a young man seeing a man whom I once considered an intelligent man. On this occasion he was drunk. His foolishness brought out all of his weakest traits. After that event, I could never admire him again. He was weakened in my eyes. All of his achievements were blurred by that experience.

On the other extreme there are men who seem to celebrate their stupidity. Today it seems as if foolishness is glorified in men. Television commercials, sitcoms, and comedians seem to revel in the idea that men are imbeciles.

Don't be foolish. Be a lifelong learner. Continue to grow, read, and become. Don't glorify stupidity. There is nothing impressive about an ignorant man.

The average millionaire reads at least one nonfiction book a month. Be a reader.

Most men become millionaires in their fifties. So at "half-time," in mid-life, reevaluate your life so that you can finish strong.

Learn the value of your wisdom and exchange it for those who don't have it yet. Wisdom is a commodity. It is exchangeable for goods. It is a currency of exchange.

> *Blessed is the man who finds wisdom, the man who gains understanding*
> *for she is more profitable than silver and yields better returns than gold.*
>
> Proverbs 3:13–14

Notice, that the commodity of true wealth is wisdom. I've known many people who have intellectual ability but lack wisdom. Some academic elitists are really just babbling fools, worth nothing of significant value. They carry on about all that they know, but when it is all said and done they are vacuous idiots.

Biblical wisdom can produce results. It has a "get-it-done" mentality. It rejects the empty ideas of smooth or soaring rhetoric. The Apostle Paul found these foolish types of dreamers in Athens.

> *While Paul was waiting for them in Athens, he was greatly distressed to*
> *see that the city was full of idols. So he reasoned in the synagogue with the*
> *Jews and the God-fearing Greeks, as well as in the marketplace day by*
> *day with those who happened to be there. A group of Epicurean and Stoic*
> *philosophers began to dispute with him.*
>
> Acts 17:16

The Athenians spent their time doing nothing but talking and arguing about the latest ideas *(Acts 17:21)*. This practice is only afforded when the country is experiencing enormous economic privilege; otherwise they would have been at work.

It is much like the "talking heads" on 24-hour news programs today. They spend all of their time talking. It seems as if they never have anything to say; but they just keep on talking. This is useless propaganda.

Spend your time on something that matters. These people need to shut up and go do something.

Chapter 14

A Husband is a Cultivator

*The Lord God took the man and put him in the Garden of Eden to work
it and take care of it.*

Genesis 2:15

To understand Man you must go back to his original design—which is to say, you must look at Adam.

God allowed the seeds in the Garden to remain dormant until He created Adam to cultivate it. *(See Genesis 2:5.)* Only after He created Man did God release the seed, shrubs, and plants to spring up. That tells us a lot about God's intentions in stewardship. God doesn't carry out His plans haphazardly. He puts everything in order.

God gave Man the employment of working the Garden. Even before Adam had a wife, he had a job. *(That is what I tell my daughters. Before a boy can date you, he has to have a job. That is God's order.)*

The word translated as *work* in Genesis 2:15 is a Hebrew word which means *to labor or dress*. The word translated as *take care of* means *to guard, preserve, protect, and celebrate*.

When God placed Adam in Eden, He established a "vocation" for Man. The word *vocation* literally means that God gave a *divinely spoken word* over him. Man is a developer and a cultivator by God's design. Deep within the desire of Man is the appetite to improve whatever he touches.

Because of this divine imprint, Man is a cultivator of Woman. A husband should improve a woman's life by being with her and spending time with her. She should feel better about herself, be more confident, and have a sense of destiny within her because of the man in her life.

Man is a developer and a cultivator by God's design.

As a cultivator, a husband should enable the woman to bear fruit. She should be productive because of his influence in her life.

Proverbs 31 speaks of a remarkable woman and it makes several important statements such as:

1.   Her husband has full confidence in her and lacks nothing of value.

2.   She brings him good, not harm, all the days of her life.

3.   She selects wool and flax and works with eager hands.

4.   She is like the merchant ships, bringing food from afar.

5.   She gets up while it is still dark. She provides food for her family.

6.   She considers a field and buys it.

7.   Out of her earnings, she plants a vineyard.

8.   She sets about her work vigorously.

9.   Her arms are strong for her tasks.

10.   She sees that her trading is profitable.

What an amazing woman. I picked up from this chapter how entrepreneurial a woman can be, so I wanted to cultivate that spirit in my wife. To do so, I changed the way that I handled our household budget.

I began to practice what I call the "Division of Ten Principle." Every dollar is easily divided into ten parts. As a believer, I know that the first dime is the Tithe. I take the Tithe and worship God with it first. The second dime, I turn and give to my wife and bless her saying, "Now, go consider a field and buy it, I know that your trading is profitable."

My wife began to consider products, to buy them, and then place them on eBay. Her returns are better than anything I could get from Wall Street! She has been averaging 20, 30, 40, and sometimes up to 100% per week on our investments.

Think about what a powerful statement it is for my wife, when she agrees with me as we worship God with the very first dime, and then I turn to her and entrust her with the second dime of all my income. My trust gives her confidence to work vigorously.

Some men never release their wives into their giftings. They have archaic attitudes of superiority toward women. Although, man is the Gate of Authority to the woman, he is to be a servant leader, not a dominator.

This idea of cultivating your wife has amazing benefits in your life. You are not trying to make her something that she is not. You are simply cultivating the deep seeds of greatness within her.

It's sad, but some women have a distorted image of themselves because their husbands are always trying to replicate them into someone that they lust for. Rather than cultivating the greatness in their wives that first attracted them, these men spend all their efforts trying to make their wives into something they are not.

A woman is beautiful when she is cultivated to be her true and best self. Who she becomes is a reflection of her husband's skill as a cultivator.

I remember counseling a woman who was devastated by her husband's infidelity. He was rude and verbally abusive to her. It was obvious that he found her very unattractive, and he was disgusted by her appearance. Amazingly, the husband was overweight and sloppy in his own right. Their marriage ended in divorce. The woman retuned for one last counseling session after their separation. I was grieved for her. Her confidence was shattered. Her self image was distorted. She was depressed.

I instructed her from the Word of God and encouraged her to change her life by reading the Proverbs 31 passage over and over until it sank into her spirit.

Within a few months, you couldn't imagine the difference in this woman's appearance. She got a job and began to succeed in her work. She lost all of her excess weight and started dressing very well. Her confidence matured. Her joy returned. She ended up marrying another man who was very successful in his business.

It wasn't long after that time that I ran into the former husband. He looked awful. He was lonely, depressed, even lost. I realized that since she was no longer there to receive his self-hatred and abuse, he had no one else to destroy but himself.

Chapter 15
The Gate for Children

He who fears the Lord has a secure fortress, and for his children it will be a refuge.

Proverbs 14:26

The father who fears the Lord is the Gate of Authority for his children. Your relationships within the protocol of authority build security in your household. Your home will become a place of safety for your children. It will always be a place of peace and rest where they can find refuge from the storms and trials of life.

His sons used to take turns holding feasts in their homes, and they would invite their three sisters to eat and drink with them. When a period of feasting had run its course, Job would send and have them purified. Early in the morning he would sacrifice a burnt offering for each of them, thinking, "Perhaps my children have sinned and cursed God in their hearts." This was Job's regular custom.

Job 1:4–5

Job was an extremely blessed man. He was so blessed that Satan accused Job of serving the Lord only for personal gain *(Job 1:9)*. Job was also a man of integrity in his speech *(Job 2:9)*.

Job's life is certainly an example of patience, yet there is something else that we can learn concerning his relationship with his ten children.

Job's relationship with his children was based upon fear—not faith.

Job's self-absorbed children would celebrate at each other's houses. After their drunkenness, Job customarily made sacrifices, thinking that his children in their inebriated states might have said something against God. A sacrifice on behalf of each child with a minimum of ten celebrations a year meant that Job made at least 100 sacrifices a year for his children.

Rather than training up his children in the way that they should go, Job formed a habit of making sacrifices on their behalf without ever correcting them. When disaster came, the children were susceptible to destruction. They all perished, and Job acknowledged that the thing that he feared the most had happened (*Job 3:25*).

The father is the Gate of Authority for his children.

So many people live in fear concerning their children. They constantly make sacrifices on behalf of them, excusing their bad behavior, never directing their steps, never disciplining them to walk in what is right. I have seen children raised in such a manner that they adopt a destructive attitude in their own lives because of their spoiled upbringing. Alcohol abuse, drug addictions, sexual promiscuity, and eating disorders are rampant in the homes of undisciplined children.

> *Discipline your son, for in that there is hope; do not be a willing party to his death.*
>
> Proverbs 19:18

The father is the Gate of Authority for his children, and proper discipline will protect his children from harm.

In 2007, an heir to one of the greatest estates in our country had a son attending college. The son's attitude was slothful and lazy. He was more interested in partying and hanging out than in studying and pursuing his education.

His father was discouraged by his son's elitist attitude, so he called and told him, "Son, you are leaving college tomorrow. You will be returning home. I have an entry-level job lined up in one of our stores, where you will be working 40 hours a week until you learn the value of getting an education to earn a living."

One week after the boy left Virginia Tech college, a mentally deranged student went on the deadliest shooting rampage ever committed by a single gunman in U.S. history. The rich young man's roommate was killed. This rich young student could have also been a casualty that day, if it were not for his father's discipline.

Dad—you are the Gate of Authority for your children. You have a responsibility to raise them in the command of the Lord. What separates a godly father from other men is his patriarchal nature to strengthen his children.

You must step up to direct your children.

This is why Abraham was chosen by God to establish an everlasting covenant. It is the defining character trait that separated him from his peers.

> *Abraham will surely become a great and powerful nation, and all nations*
> *on earth will be blessed through him. For I have chosen him, so that he*
> *will direct his children and his household after him to keep the way of the*

Lord by doing what is right and just, so that the Lord will bring about for
Abraham what he has promised him.

Genesis 18:18–19

In this passage, *to direct* means *to give charge to, to command, to commission, or to give order*. What distinguished Abraham in the eyes of God was his willingness to be the Gate of Authority over his home.

This is vital. You must step up to direct your children. You must be willing to oversee them and give them order in life. Few parents are willing to do this. Any excursion to a department store will illustrate this point. You'll find parents who are commanded by their children, rather than vice-versa, and children who tell their parents how to spend their incomes to satisfy their every little whim.

Job was a great man, and he had a wonderful personal relationship with God, but he failed to direct his children. Abraham, on the other hand, had command over his children, and God choose him because He needed a man who could firmly establish His covenant on the Earth.

Abraham directed Isaac, Isaac directed Jacob, and thus God's covenant was established with Abraham, Isaac, and Jacob.

Do you know that Abraham's progeny extends to you?

You are a son or daughter of Abraham because of his willingness to direct his children (*Galatians 3:7–9, 29*).

Father—you are responsible for your children's education and spiritual teaching. *That's right—you heard me.* You can't just farm out your responsibility to train up your child in the way that he should go to your wife. *You* must take the mantle of leadership as the instructor to your children.

When your children go to school, you should review the lessons that they are learning. When you go to church, you should discuss spiritual things with them. Make them comfortable to talk about spiritual things. Don't forfeit your place as the teacher and spiritual instructor of your family.

Chapter 16

Closing the Gate to the Devil

But I tell you that anyone who looks at a woman lustfully has already committed adultery with her in his heart.

Matthew 5:28

Father—do you realize the vital importance of your role as the Gatekeeper to your family?

One day, I received a disturbing phone call from a man in my church. He told me how he was secretly struggling with pornography. As I listened to him, a multitude of scriptures came to mind. During the conversation, I picked up on the fact that he had a flippant attitude toward this sin. He tried to excuse it away by saying, "I don't care who you are, everyone struggles with it."

I boldly asked, "Do you know that you are committing adultery?"

"No," he answered, "I haven't committed adultery. That's different."

I answered back, "Jesus said that when you gaze upon a woman with lust for her body, you have committed adultery in your heart."

He was silent.

Then I continued, "Proverbs 22:14 states, 'The mouth of an adulteress is a deep pit; he who is under the Lord's wrath will fall into it.' Adultery is not the cause of a fallen relationship with God.

It's simply a manifestation that your heart is already away from God? Your problem is that you don't love Jesus."

Nothing fazed this man. Then the Holy Spirit directed me to teach him about the Gate of Authority. "You are the Gate of Authority to your family. If you allow the spirit of voyeuristic adultery to enter your life, you are essentially saying, 'Devil, have your way with my children in this arena. Go ahead, I have opened the Gate of Authority to my home. I give you my permission to enter.'"

At that point, the man cried out in repentance. The truth set him free from his addictive lust. This principle empowered him to overcome his flesh, and he built up a hedge of protection around his family following that conversation.

What you do in secret will be shouted from the rooftops.

Most men have a fallacious belief that their secret sins are their own business—that they will hurt no one—they are simply a personal thing. Remember "The Closet Principle:" *What you do in secret will be shouted from the rooftops.*

Furthermore, the Book of Job shows that there is a direct correlation between a man's willingness to lust for a woman and his wife becoming a servant to another man!

> *I made a covenant with my eyes not to look lustfully at a girl. For what is man's lot from God above, his heritage from the Almighty on high. Is it not ruin for the wicked, disaster for those who do wrong? Does he not see my ways and count my every step?*

If my steps have turned from the path, if my heart has been led by my eyes, or if my hands have been defiled, then may others eat what I have sown, and may my crops be uprooted.

If my heart has been enticed by a woman, or if I have lurked at my neighbor's door, then may my wife grind another man's grain, and may other men sleep with her. For that would have been shameful, a sin to be judged. It is a fire that burns to Destruction; it would have uprooted my harvest.

Job 31:1–4, 7–12

A man causes self-destruction by opening his eye gate to lust.

David is an example of a man who looked lustfully upon another woman and the repercussions for his family were disastrous.

In the spring, at the time when kings go off to war, David sent Joab out with the king's men and the whole Israelite army. They destroyed the Ammonites and besieged Rabbah. But David remained in Jerusalem.

II Samuel 11:1–5

Notice the phrase, "In the spring, at the time when kings go off to war." Every man has a cause to fight for, but unless he knows what it is, he will always fight for the wrong thing.

David laid down his hunger for risk taking. I have noticed that often a man is attracted to adultery out of sheer boredom. It often brings a sense of risk and adventure into his otherwise dull existence.

Such was the case with David.

You know the story. David walked up onto his balcony and began to gaze upon the beautiful Bathsheba. Then he took his lust another next step further. He summoned her to his bed.

After David was told that Bathsheba was pregnant he began to devise a wicked scheme. Proverbs 12:20 says, "There is deceit in the heart of those who plot evil."

Acting out of lust and fear, David summoned Bathsheba's husband to return from the battlefield. He expected Uriah to sleep with his wife so that the truth of her pregnancy would be covered up.

Think about how wicked the scheme was. David was willing to have his own flesh and blood falsely adopted and raised by one of his soldiers, rather than acknowledge the truth. In a sense, David was giving up his son's life. This seed of deception later cost him the life of his child!

Uriah, whose name means, "God is my flame," proved to be an honorable man. He showed himself faithful to the righteous cause of his country and was unwilling to sleep in his house with his wife while he was on leave from his companions on the field of battle.

> *Uriah said to David, "The ark and Israel and Judah are staying in tents,*
> *and my master Joab and my lord's men are camped in the open fields.*
> *How could I go to my house to eat and drink and lie with my wife? As*
> *surely as you live, I will not do such a thing!"*
> *II Samuel 11:11*

As shown in the life of David, the spirit of adultery is separated from the spirit of murder by a very thin line. That is why so many adulterous relationships end up with someone being killed.

David's evil plot failed to cover his sins, and he accepted a murderous spirit.

David sent Uriah back unknowingly carrying his own death warrant to Joab. It was a note giving orders to expose Uriah to the heat of battle and withdraw from him allowing the enemy to kill him.

After the deed was done, the prophet Nathan came to David and asked for a judgment on a matter. Read the story in II Samuel 12. Nathan allowed David to ensnare himself with his own words, and then he declared, "You are the man!"

This is very important, so don't gloss over this part of the story.

Nathan went on to prophesy, "You killed [Uriah] with the sword of the Ammonites. Now, therefore, the sword [of the Ammonites] will never depart from your house, because you despised me and took the wife of Uriah the Hittite to be your own" *(II Samuel 12:9–10)*.

The Ammonites were a constant enemy of the people of Israel. David used their wickedness to do his murderous deed. The Ammonites were also an incestuous people. They habitually married among their own relatives.

The prophet declared, "Out of your own household calamity will come upon you" *(II Samuel 12:11)*.

In II Samuel 13, a son of David, Amnon, became obsessed with his sister Tamar. He devised a scheme to rape her. Once he disgraced her, all of his emotions then turned to bitter hatred, stronger than the lust he had had for her before. The consequences were devastating for the poor teenage girl who was raped and defiled. She became a desolate woman, never able to marry, and remaining barren for the rest of her life.

Nathan's prophesy came to pass. David opened the Gate of Authority to his own household with his wicked plot against Uriah, and it began to come back into his own home.

The rape of Tamar set in motion another layer of the recompense. Tamar's brother Absalom, beloved son of David, devised a plot to avenge his sister, killing Amnon. Absalom later became the usurper of David's throne. Nathan's prophesy came to full fruition. Out of David's own household came incest, murder, and destruction.

As great a man as David was, as much as he accomplished in his lifetime, as significant as his throne was even to the Messianic line, he failed as a father.

Of all the giants, enemies, and battles that David fought and won, he lost the most important battle—the battle for his home.

Speaking of an adulterous woman, David's son, Solomon, writes, "Many are the victims she has brought down; her slain are a mighty throng" (Proverbs 7:26).

The collateral damage of adultery cannot be measured. It is overwhelming to see its destructive force and the forfeiture of wealth it causes (see Proverbs 5:10), not to mention, the lives of countless children that are ruined by the continual shadow of shame.

Although David was able to repent and renew his commitment to the Lord, the shame and repercussions of his sin follow him to this day.

How to Lead Others With Authority

Chapter 17

How to Lead Others

For I myself am a man under authority, with soldiers under me. I tell this one, "Go," and he goes; and that one, "Come," and he comes. I say to my servant, "Do this," and he does it.

Matthew 8:9

You know that the rulers of the Gentiles lord it over them, and their high officials exercise authority over them. Not so with you. Instead, whoever wants to become great among you must be your servant.

Matthew 20:25

The centurion knew how to approach the authority above him. He knew also that he had been placed in a position of authority so that he might lead others.

Following the proper protocol of authority above you gives you the confidence to lead those under you. The centurion was given his position not to arbitrarily rule over or to dictate to people, but to allow what was above him to flow down to what was beneath him.

When you have protocol working in your life, your confidence to lead comes directly from the work that you are doing. Jesus demonstrated this by completing what His Father had called him to do.

You granted [me] authority over all people… I have brought you glory on earth by completing the work you gave me to do.

John 17:2, 4 (paraphrased)

The reason that we have authority is to accomplish the work that we are assigned. What good is authority except for the purpose of administering it to complete a task?

Some leaders don't administer authority beneath them very well. They are duplicitous when it comes to directing people. This causes an insecurity within their ranks.

During Jesus' ministry on Earth, He demonstrated how a leader should protect those under Him. In John 17:12, He reported to the Father, "While I was with them, I protected [my disciples] and kept them safe by that name you gave me. None has been lost except the one doomed to destruction so that Scripture would be fulfilled."

Jesus protected His disciples and kept them safe through the integrity of His Word and His use of His name.

Those who are under your care of leadership must hear from you. They cannot follow what they have not heard. Jesus said, "My sheep hear my voice and the voice of a stranger they will not follow" *(John 10:4–5).*

When I started my first church, it was my habit to pray everyday, "Lord, I need wisdom and insight and understanding on how to lead this church." It seemed as if everyday, I would receive instruction directly from God.

We set a course to build a new facility. I prayed and asked God for insight. I had never built a church facility, so I needed His help.

One day, I was greatly concerned about the way the ceiling in the auditorium was going to turn out. I could see that it would have a very negative affect on the room. So, I began to pray about it. That night I had a dream about the ceiling. I saw how it should be built. I awakened and drew it out on a piece of paper.

> *I remembered my songs in the night. My heart mused and my spirit inquired.*
>
> *Psalm 77:6*

The next morning I showed up at the construction site early. When the craftsman arrived, I said, "You know, I was thinking about the ceiling. I'm not really happy with the way it will turn out. What if we did this?" I showed him what I had drawn on paper.

He exclaimed, "That will be a lot better than the way the architect has it drawn!"

I said, "Go ahead. Do it like this."

"Won't this require a change order?" he asked. "Does your building committee need to meet? My crew will be here in a few minutes. I don't want to send them home."

I reassured him. "Don't worry about it. The 'committee' and I met last night."

My point is that the Spirit of God above me was instructing me, and in turn I entrusted those beneath me to do the job.

I left that church a few years later to become the executive pastor at a mega-church. As it was my habit, I would pray daily, "Lord, give me wisdom and insight and understanding about the church."

Nothing—I heard nothing from the Lord.

Day after day, I prayed this prayer. I heard nothing at all.

One day, I was so disturbed about not hearing from the Lord that I wrote down five specific questions that I knew that the church was dealing with. I prayed for the answers to those questions. Still I heard nothing.

I was so distraught about it that I went to my pastor and asked him to go to lunch. I was considering that I must be out of the will of God for my life since I was not hearing from God anymore.

During the lunch, my pastor began to talk. He said, "Neil, I've been thinking about this…" When he did, he answered the first question that I had asked the Lord that morning. Then he went on, "And, I've been thinking about what we should do about this…" He answered the second question. He continued to answer every question in the order that I had prayed about them earlier. Then I realized what was going on. I was a man under authority! God was not going to speak to me *around* my leader. He was going to speak to me *through* my leader.

Only after I left that position to start my second church, did I begin to hear directly from the Lord again concerning all the different areas of the church. I learned a valuable lesson that has helped me tremendously to understand how God speaks *to* and *through* leadership.

I wish I had known that earlier in my ministry.

God will not speak around your leader. He will speak through your leader.

I have always recruited people to serve in my ministry. I recruited a high school football coach to become my youth pastor. While he was serving with me, we built the largest youth ministry in the state of Alabama. I recruited a banker to become a business administrator. I recruited an engineer/ship builder, and he became a strategic planner for the church. Then I recruited a house painter to become the children's minister at our church.

For two years, this man served faithfully and was a remarkable staff member. In those two years, he was the best staff member I had ever hired. Until one day, a bitter root was deposited within him.

His father had visited our church. Later I found out that his father had begun to compare him to me. He pointed out how young and inexperienced I was, and how mature and capable his son was. That's when things changed. It also turned out that the youth pastor began to murmur against me as well. The two consoled each other in their rebellion against my authority.

I noticed the difference in them for the first time, when I began to see "special" prayer meetings were being called for the children's ministry leadership team. I went to one and sat in the back of the room. My heart was grieved within me. The spiritual climate in the room wasn't in harmony with my spirit.

I couldn't believe it. Most of the people who had submitted to him had been saved, or healed, or had a marriage restored under my ministry. There was even a barren woman who conceived a child after I had prayed with her and her husband.

One day, I approached the children's pastor and said, "I believe that you want to pastor. I want to help you—if you do it the right way."

He assured me that he had no intention to do so. He looked me straight in the eye and lied.

At a staff meeting, I asked him to check on a bus that I had seen for sale at another church. A couple of weeks went by, and I asked about it. He simply said, "Oh, it's not something that you really want."

A few weeks later, he resigned.

He started a church just a couple of miles from our location. One day when I drove by the leased building that he had acquired, sure enough, that bus was sitting in the parking lot.

He pirated all the staff that I had entrusted under his care. He persuaded them to leave the church and follow him. He never spoke openly against me. He simply planted doubts and suspicions about me, suggesting that somehow God had "revealed" something about me to him, that he couldn't say.

I can't tell you how devastating it was to have a staff member do such a thing—but more importantly, how devastating it was to the families that left with him. The collateral damage caused by the usurping of my authority in that church can't be measured. Lives were destroyed. Some were embittered. Some were lost.

When you depart from the protocol of authority, you step out from under the umbrella of protection and become harassed by spiritual forces that are lawbreakers.

I will say that a couple of years later, the church pirate finally repented to me privately and then confessed publicly. "I gave myself over to deceptive spirits," he admitted. "I knew better, but I did it anyway."

When you depart from the protocol of authority, you step out from under the umbrella of protection and become harassed by spiritual forces that are lawbreakers.

When Jesus landed and saw a large crowd, he had compassion on them,
because they were like sheep without a shepherd...

Mark 6:34

Israel had an established spiritual system of governance, which was supposed to be administered by the Levitical lineage; however, they began to follow a branch of religious-minded legalists called the Pharisees.

The problem with the Pharisees was that they were not the God-ordained spiritual authorities. They were men who established traditions and formalities to try to nullify the Word of God. They were much more like a political party rather than a spiritual administration.

When Jesus had finished saying these things, the crowds were amazed at
his teaching, because he taught as one who had authority, and not as
their teachers of the law.

Matthew 7:28

The Pharisees were meticulous in points of the Law, yet they lacked all the authority within it. Their spiritual deficiency of authority caused them to feel enormous insecurity. Because of their lack of authority, they began to overemphasize their importance. They had to exercise control and oppression over people in order to feel important.

I've seen this hundreds of times in businesses, ministries, and even families. When leaders lack the confidence of their positions they become delusional and controlling. The use tactics of intimidation and manipulation, rather than inspiring people to follow them in confidence.

You should avoid these people at all costs. They are dangerous in their deception. They are cultish in their delusions. They are led by evil spirits, controlling and oppressing people's wills. Don't give place to their leadership in your life.

God will give you authority as you follow proper protocol. You will have the confidence to lead those under you and allow what is above you to flow down to those beneath you. Your confidence to lead will come directly from the work you are doing, and you will complete what the Father has called you to do.

Chapter 18

Give Clear Instruction

The proverbs of Solomon son of David, king of Israel...

Proverbs 1:1

I love reading Proverbs every day. Years ago, I learned to discipline myself to read one chapter each day. Reading Proverbs ensures that I will gain wisdom, discipline, insight, prudence, knowledge, and discretion.

Solomon received instruction from his father David, the king of Israel, and in the Book of Proverbs, Solomon passed on the lessons to us. These valuable insights help us walk through life with a standard that is above the norm.

Obviously there are sobering warnings about adultery. There is also wise instruction concerning our finances, leadership lessons, family relations, and managing friendships.

Receiving and giving instruction is a skill. In order to lead others you must master the art of communicating.

Remember the centurion said, "I am a man under authority therefore, I tell this one, 'Go,' and he goes; and that one, 'Come,' and he comes. I say to my servant, 'Do this,' and he does it."

The centurion understood how to give instructions. He knew that instructions should be specific. To one he said, "Go," to another he said, "Come," and still to another he said, "Do this."

Leaders must clearly communicate their instructions in order for their followers to be able to run with them.

> *Write down the revelation and make it plain on tablets so that a herald*
> *may run with it.*
>
> *Habakkuk 2:2*

Those who follow you cannot see what you see unless you clearly communicate.

Growing up, I struggled to communicate with my stepfather. He and I were never on the same page. He assumed that I knew what he knew. When we worked together on the farm, around the equipment, he would get very frustrated with me because I didn't know what he wanted. My relationship with him never connected. He and my older brother got along very well. They continue to have a father-son relationship to this day, even though our mother divorced him more than twenty-eight years ago. But somehow, my stepfather and I never could make that connection.

When you are leading someone, do not assume that they know what you know.

You must learn to communicate well in order for people to follow you. Also, as a leader, learn to speak your words clearly. Don't mumble. Mumbling shows a lack of confidence and makes you appear as if you you are weak-minded.

Our society has become very casual in its conversation. Email and text messages have created informal and loose communication. Be careful. Don't allow this informality to drift into your speaking.

Also, don't adopt the habit that is so prevalent today of bantering and talking over others when they are speaking. Your words are important. Don't waste them by speaking when another person can't hear you.

Speaking the right words is more important than speaking many words.

As a leader, you should encourage others to speak clearly back to you. If you did not hear what someone said, ask him to repeat it to you, and be sure you heard and understood his point of view.

> *A word aptly spoken is like apples of gold in settings of silver.*
>
> Proverbs 25:11

Above all else, remember that speaking the *right* words is more important than speaking *many* words.

I work hard to clearly communicate. I invest time in learning new words each day so that I can have a better vocabulary to make appropriate conversation. Please don't get me wrong. Some people enlarge their vocabularies only for show and not for clarity. What good is a word if the hearer doesn't understand what you are saying?

Flowery rhetoric is useless if it is only empty words revealing a vacuous mind. Men follow men who speak few, but powerful and honest, words.

Steps to Communicating Clearly

1.   Give specific direction. The centurion said, "Go," "Come," and "Do this."

2.   Speak clearly.

3.   Watch over your words and make sure that your subordinates follow your instructions.

I've learned the hard way that people do what you inspect, not necessarily what you expect. You must be willing to follow up your command and "watch over it."

Another mistake many leaders make is that they are too naive to trust people without any verification of their honesty or ability. When I was young and naive I trusted people, now that I am matured and wiser, I test people *before* I trust them.

I have always looked for opportunities to instruct my staff during unstructured times. While driving, during casual time, or during a round of golf, I try to take the time to speak to them about principles that will lay the ground work for leadership in their lives.

Don't assume that those underneath you hear what you have heard. They must hear from you. You must develop a communication rhythm with those under you.

This is especially true when it comes to leading children.

Teach them to your children, talking about them when you sit at home and when you walk along the road, when you lie down and when you get up.

Deuteronomy 11:19

I've heard many great preachers say, "Faith is caught rather than taught."

I can't disagree more. We should never assume that our children will "catch" what we believe. In fact, that kind of mentality explains why so many second-generation Christians have wandered from the faith.

We must communicate clearly for people to follow our leadership.

Chapter 19
Transferring Your Authority

Jesus came to them and said, "All authority in heaven and on earth has been given to me. Therefore go and make disciples."

Matthew 28:18–19

Authority must flow through leadership. The leadership above us must be willing to extend their power and influence to us so that we are empowered to act on their behalf. But we also must be willing to release those under our leadership to receive the same empowerment for their protection and benefit.

The centurion demonstrated how much trust he had in the system of authority when he said, "I am a man under authority, I tell this man to 'Go,' and he goes, this man 'Come,' and he comes, another 'Do this,' and he does it."

He understood that the entire Roman Empire existed to back up his words of authority.

Think about how powerful it was for this man to operate in the established system of authority. The system would have broken down if he, and others like him, didn't understand their place in the protocol.

Unfortunately, that is where we find most men today. They are ignorant, or they have been deceived into thinking that they do not have authority and that their words don't matter. The collateral damage of this error is heart-wrenching.

Subordinates will never have confidence in you, if you do not transfer authority to them.

Subordinates, whether employees, congregants, or family members, will never have a sense of security and confidence in your leadership, if you do not transfer authority to them.

In the early days of my leadership, I didn't know how to make the transfer of my authority. I failed to empower my employees. My wishy-washy attitude felt like a limp-wristed handshake. The gesture was there, but the confidence was weak.

Because of my successful ministry to youth, a few couples in my first church asked me to conduct a series of teachings that would help them raise their teenagers. My children were very young at the time, and even though I had pastored teens, I had never raised any. My lack of confidence in my own teaching glared through. I stumbled and bumbled through the first class. Embarrassed, I went to prayer. I prayed, "God how am I going to help these parents? They came to hear me teach them something to help them through these difficult years. What am I going to do?"

I began to realize that my teaching wasn't limited to my personal experience, but it was based upon the higher authority of my life, namely God. I began to see that I was empowered to teach principles to those parents and equip them with the Word of God.

The next week was remarkably different. As I began to teach, it seemed as if everyone in the room leaned forward to engage in what I was teaching. The teaching drew them closer. By the end of the class, they were empowered! They received a transfer of authority.

I've seen this principle work on more than one field of contest.

Great coaches know how to empower the leaders on the field to make decisions in the times of battle. If circumstances and conditions warrant an adjustment in the play, the team leader must be empowered to be decisive. If the leader doesn't have the confidence that he will be backed up in his decision, then he will never have the confidence to lead on the field.

I've also seen this in the business arena. Employees who are meeting customers face to face must have the confidence that they are being backed up by management, otherwise, they will reflect an atmosphere of distrust. Banks are notorious for this attitude. It is as if the tellers are always on shifting sands, unstable, and insecure.

I was recently dealing with a large corporation concerning a failed product. Customer service was inept to help me at first. Relentless, I worked through the company's system of hierarchy until I finally found someone who had the confidence to make a decision. It was amazing how easy it was to fix the problem once someone had the confidence to actually do it. Three wasted hours on the phone could have been eliminated in less than 5 minutes, if the first person I had talked to had been empowered to make a decision.

Children pick up on this protocol quickly. If you want to protect your children from the temptations of drugs, alcohol, and other vices, you must empower them with your authority. They must feel that you are backing them up. They must know that you have their backs.

Think about how powerful this principle regarding the protocol of authority is at work in us when it is applied to the forgiveness of sins.

> *If you forgive anyone his sins, they are forgiven; if you do not forgive*
> *them, they are not forgiven.*
>
> John 20:23

Amazing isn't it? God has transfered His authority to the grass-roots in your field of contest. You actually have been empowered to forgive sins.

God's authority flows through the protocol of leadership to you, so that you may also release it to others.

> *I will give you the keys of the kingdom of heaven; whatever you bind on earth will be bound in heaven, and whatever you loose on earth will be loosed in heaven.*
>
> Matthew 16:19

Jesus transferred the keys of the kingdom of Heaven to us so that we have the ability to bind and loose. Keys indicate that you have the power to open or close access points, such as gates or doors.

Jesus transferred the keys of the kingdom of Heaven to us.

At our home, I have enough confidence in my wife and children to give them keys to our home and automobiles. They have been given the same ability that I have to open doors.

That is what Jesus did when He gave us the keys to Heaven and Earth. We have the personal ability to open and close these doors of access.

What we must do is transfer that ability to those who serve beneath us; otherwise, they will never have the confidence to practice proper protocol.

Jesus demonstrated this transfer when He empowered His disciples.

After this the Lord appointed seventy-two others and sent them two by two ahead of him to every town and place where he was about to go.

Luke 10:1

Jesus sent them ahead of Him into the towns. They exercised their authority to prepare for His coming.

The seventy-two returned with joy and said, "Lord, even the demons submit to us in your name."

Luke 10:17

"Even the demons submit…" This empowerment came to the disciples because Jesus had transfered His authority to them through His name. They exercised His authority and even the demons had to submit to them.

If you will carefully look at the life of Jesus, He walked as a man in the power of the Holy Spirit and exercised the authority that His Father had given Him. This same Jesus transfered His authority to us. Now to make the cycle complete, we must transfer our authority to those who are under us—in our churches, in our homes, and in the workplace.

Chapter 20

Men of Authority, Men of Action

When there are no men, be a man.

—*Rabbi Hillel*

Let there be no doubt: your manhood is in question. Society wants you to conform to its pattern of a weak-minded, passive, "Momma's-boy" metro-sexual. Don't do it. Don't think that you have to check in your manhood to fulfill God's design for your life. In fact, it's just the opposite. God made you a man—so be one.

If you are submitted to the Lordship of Jesus Christ, you are positioned within the protocol of authority to exercise authority for that which you have responsibility. You have also been empowered to transfer that authority to those who are under your care.

As a man under authority, you have a legitimate right to use His power.

We are facing troubled times. These times call for action. We need your leadership. We need men who are courageous enough to stand up and take their proper place in manhood.

It is time we step into our proper role as men and stand tall with conviction. It is time to step up to the challenge. It is time that men become men.

Epilogue

My wife Kay and I began the year of 2008 with a twenty-one-day Daniel fast. We sensed God was calling us to a new endeavor. As I prayed during the twenty-one days, I had a strong conviction that I was not finished. Kay and I agreed to press on with the fast. We took a week off, then started another twenty-one days.

During that second fast, a ministry partner of mine, Tom Yandell, contacted me. He sensed I had a message that needed to get out and wanted to offer his services to help me. I replied that we would talk soon.

I had a consulting meeting scheduled in Tulsa, Oklahoma for the spring of '08. I asked Tom to pick me up at the airport.

Tulsa has always played an important role in my life. Not only is it where I am from but it is also where the Lord has specifically directed my ministry steps. In fact, five major changes in my ministry happened while I was in prayer in Tulsa. This trip proved to be one of those significant times.

When my plane touched down on the tarmac at Tulsa, the Spirit of the Lord deposited within me a strategy. It was an impartation of knowledge *(1 Corinthians 2:6–13)*. Over the next few hours, Tom and I began to plan and strategize in minute detail.

We named this strategy Fivestar Man.

This strategy draws upon the greatness of man. I live with the deep conviction that there is more in you than you have expected. I believe in God-given gifts and I believe God has deposited intrinsic value and abilities deep within you. Your abilities, resources, and talents are needed in this time.

> *The purposes of a man's heart are deep waters, but a man of understanding draws them out.*
>
> Proverbs 20:5

Fivestar Man is a multifaceted approach that motivates men to live a passionate life—a life of adventure, filled with entrepreneurial drive, gallantry, faithfulness, and legacy-driven action. It is a network of men who literally feel called to be something more than usual.

> *From one* **man** *he made every nation of* **men**, *that they should inhabit the whole earth; and he determined the times set for them and the exact places where they should live.*
>
> Acts 17:26

**To become personally involved and
learn more about our strategy, visit us at:**
www.fivestarman.com

About The Author

Neil Kennedy discovered the truths about The Centurion Principle, God's Currency, and The Seven Laws Which Govern Increase and Order out of necessity, from the principles he found in God's Word and from his own personal experience.

Neil worked as a heavy-machine operator in a coalmine in Oklahoma before attending Central Bible College in Springfield, Missouri, where he majored in Pastoral Studies. Working his way through college, Neil discovered that even his job as a salesman in a local carwash would give him insight into God's Word and His principles.

After finishing college and serving as a youth minister, Neil felt the Lord calling him to step out and pioneer Eastern Shore Christian Center in Mobile, Alabama. Growing the congregation from five people to 500, God then led Neil to step down from his position as Senior Pastor to become Executive Pastor at Church On The Move in Tulsa, Oklahoma. His experiences there allowed him to help develop the inner-workings of one of America's fastest-growing mega-churches, where he was responsible for the entire pastoral care department, overseeing the needs of more than 10,000 members each week.

In 2001, armed with instruction from the Word and the practical knowledge he had gained, Neil once again felt the Lord directing him to pioneer a church. Obeying the Lord's call, he stepped out and founded Celebrate Family Church, in Orlando, Florida.

Neil's practical insight and straight-forward communication style have inspired thousands to take the necessary steps to realize their God-given potential. Neil's expertise makes him a highly-sought-after speaker and consultant to churches and businesses alike, and to anyone who wants to increase and achieve all that God has for them.

Neil now travels each week, ministering in churches and conducting seminars across America. Neil's burning desire is to challenge pastors, church congregations, and individuals to fulfill God's purposes for themselves.

Neil has served on numerous boards, committees, and strategy forums, including the U.S. Missions Board, the Decade of Harvest Task Force, the Evangelism Task Force, and the Dove-Award-winning musical group 4-Him.

Neil Kennedy has the mission of teaching, equipping and funding church endeavors. His specialties include:

Church Planting—developing and helping new works to go from the ground up,

"Turn-Around" Churches—ministering to churches who've let tradition slow their momentum and find themselves irrelevant in today's world, and

"Next-Level" churches—assisting pastors who, for whatever reason, have hit a barrier in their growth they just can't seem to break through.

Neil and his wife, Kay, have three children, Alexandra, Chase, and Courtney, and they reside in Fairhope, Alabama.

Made in the USA
Charleston, SC
24 September 2011